FAITH
ON
TRIAL

FAITH ON TRIAL

Robert Tilton

Robert Tilton Ministries
Dallas, Texas

FAITH ON TRIAL
ISBN 0-914307-81-9
Copyright ©1989 by Robert Tilton Ministries
First Printing September, 1989

Published by Robert Tilton Ministries
P.O. Box 819000, Dallas, Texas 75381-9000
(Canadian Address:
P.O. Box 4900, Vancouver,
British Columbia, V6B 4A6)
Printed in the United States of America
All Rights Reserved
No Reproduction Without Permission
Editor: Kathryn P. Ingley
Cover Design: David Wilson

Contents

You can overcome every trial of your faith, because Christ defeated Satan's power and authority at Calvary.

Preface 7
I. Why Is Your Faith On Trial? 17
II. Why Should You Be Happy When
    Your Faith Is Tried? 37
III. What Happens To Your Faith During
    a Trial? 47
IV. What Will Jesus Do For You In
    a Trial? 59
V. What Can You Do For Yourself
    During a Trial? 69
VI. How Does the Trial of Your
    Faith Teach Patience? 75
VII. How Can You Be Victorious
    in a Trial? 83
VIII. When Is the Apparent Failure
    of Your Faith Victory? 95
IX. How Others Overcame 99
X. Overcome By Vowing and Giving 111

Preface

When times are tough and you are walking through a fiery trial, use your faith and trust God to perform His Word.

God is your champion. No matter how severe your trials, how big your troubles, how impossible the situation, or how helpless you feel, He will win your case. All you have to do is trust Him, and you can do that if you will remember four things about Him:

- He loves you
- He is faithful
- He never fails or loses
- He never changes

Marte and I have faced many trials, and we have found these characteristics of God to be absolutely true. We stand in utter confidence upon His Word because we have come to really know Him. Whenever our faith is tried, we continue to do what He says in His Word; and God always does what He says He will do (Isaiah 55:11). He has never failed us.

When God told us to build a family church in Farmers Branch in north Dallas, we sold our tent, trailer, and truck and came to Farmers Branch with $300 and all our belongings in a four-by-eight trailer.

After several days of searching for a suitable building, we leased a local YMCA building, and on March 7, 1976, I preached my first sermon in Farmers Branch to Marte, our two children, and three other people. Every Sunday morning when it seemed no other cars were turning into the parking lot, I would pray, "Thank you, Father, that this church is growing according to Acts 13:44, and almost everyone in town will come."

The three hundred dollars did not go far, and our faith was on trial; but we continued to do the Word of God and to trust Him.

Before long, many more people were coming to Word of Faith Family Church. Our little congregation grew quickly and we soon needed another building. After several months of searching, we leased a run-down warehouse on Interstate 35 on the west side of town.

We sweltered through a few July Sundays and then the congregation began pleading for air conditioning. The duct work alone would have cost $400 which we didn't have. I did some ''horse trading'' to get an air conditioner, and Marte and I, along with some dedicated members, did much of the installation work.

After three months we offered to buy the building, but the bank refused to sell. The city code required 100 parking spaces, but the church had only 12. I went to the City Council meeting and pressed for a delay in the fulfillment of this requirement. Eventually the bank sold us the building, but we could not buy adjoining parcels for expansion.

Again our faith was on trial. We knew we were doing exactly what God wanted us to do, but we kept running into barriers. Times were tough and life was full of difficulties, but we kept trusting God because He is able to do exceedingly abundantly above all we could ask or think (Ephesians 3:20).

Shortly, a better piece of property with better options turned up at the junction of I-35 and LBJ Freeway. Formal ground breaking took place in the summer of 1979. The membership had grown to about 1500 then and they wanted to see a church go up after the ground was broken. But we had to pour 69 piers 24 feet deep and 40 inches in diameter before we could set a concrete slab on top of it. The people kept looking for a building. They didn't know that we had poured $60,000 worth of concrete into the holes.

Our faith was sorely tried again. Each step we have taken for God has required our total commitment, spiritually, mentally, physically, and materially. We have found that we cannot move forward until we make that commitment.

Our congregation was impatient and observers criticized the slow progress of the building, but we were out of money. Marte and I sold our house and gave the proceeds to build God's house. We continued to pray over the "vacant lot" with its $60,000 holes in the ground. As we prayed, the "ribs" of the building appeared and we again ran short of money. But we continued to do God's Word and to pray over those "dry bones" which soon took on the look and life of a church building.

After more than $4 million and 18 months, we moved into our new Garden Sanctuary in October 1980 and our membership had swelled to 2,000. Our faith in God had defeated Satan's attacks against this ministry. We had won the case and were victorious in the trial of our faith.

Perhaps you are undergoing serious difficulties and trials and are wondering if you have enough faith to overcome. Stop worrying and be happy. Start rejoicing. You have all the faith you need. You have the right stuff. You have what it takes but you must use it. God gave it to you so that you could trust Him to do what He says He will do. He has given every one of us a measure of faith and that measure is all we will ever need (Romans 12:3; Luke 17:5-6).

Who has more faith? Someone like Elijah who challenged 450 false prophets, called down fire from Heaven, trusted God to use a raven and a starving widow to feed him, or a toddler who pulls to his feet and takes his first steps to daddy? Neither has more than the other. Each used as much faith as was necessary for the task at hand. The toddler lives by faith; he depends entirely upon his parents for survival, and he trusts them to care for him. God did not ask the toddler to call down fire from heaven; He asked Elijah whose faith had been well tempered by many trials to do that. Elijah learned to trust God to do what He said He would do.

Even when times are tough and you don't see the way out, you still have all the faith you need. The problem is that some of you let negative thinking and unbelief encrust your faith like barnacles on a ship that make it drag in the water.

Like those barnacles, negative thinking and unbelief make your faith sluggish. Satan adds a few more barnacles of his own by placing all sorts of frustrations and impossible situations in your life. Then when you are weighted down, the pressure is on and you don't see a solution, the devil is right there with an easy answer. He entices you to take what seems to be a sure-fire escape: give up on God and take control yourself, excessive eating or sleeping, illness, alcohol or drug dependencies, crime, an invitation to walk on the wild side, withdrawal from society, insanity, and even religious service.

But it is important that you keep the barnacles scraped off your faith because it is your faith that enables you to trust God. It is your faith that enables you to live triumphantly here in this life (Matthew 9:29). It is your faith that will bring you praise, glory, and honor (I Peter 1:7).

When you face impossible situations and problems, you must realize that it is your *faith* that is on trial. Just as you have character, you have faith and it will be tested. For example, honesty is a part of your character; and practically every day your honesty is tested in small ways. Did the cashier give you too much change? Did you take office supplies for personal use?

> Unless you are honest in small matters, you won't be in large ones. If you cheat even a little, you won't be honest with greater responsibilities. And if you are untrustworthy about worldly wealth, who will trust you with the true riches of heaven?
>
> Luke 16:10-11 (TLB)

In a similar way, God strengthens your faith daily to prepare you for the impossible situations and trials that Satan brings against you. But always it is your faith that is on trial—not you. Satan knows that if you keep the barnacles of negative thinking and unbelief scraped off, He cannot win because God has ordained that a bit

of faith no larger than a grain of mustard seed—
about this size • —is all that is necessary for you
to win your case (Luke 17:5-6).

You see, faith works by love and love casts
out fear (Galatians 5:6; I John 4:18). When you
are not afraid, it is easy to trust God. Over and
over in the Word, God says, ''Fear not, for I am
with you'' (Isaiah 41:10 TLB). He even asks who
can be against you if He is on your side (Romans
8:31). God is *your* champion. He wants you to
triumph. That's why He has given you faith so
that you can trust Him without fear. That's also
why Satan tries your faith tempting you with situations, pressures, etc. not to trust God or, in
other words, step out of faith. Using his lies,
Satan even accuses you of not having faith in
God.

In Matthew 7, Jesus said that the person who
heard His Word and did it was like a man who
built his house on a rock.

> And the rain descended, and the
> floods came, and the winds blew
> [trials], and beat upon that house; and
> it *fell not*: for it was founded upon a
> rock [the Word of God].
>
> Matthew 7:25

When stormy trials beat upon your life you may
be tempted to give in, but if you continue to do
God's Word, you will win. Failure to practice
God's Word—not the storms—is what destroys
you.

Several years ago God told me in the middle of the night that many of His people fail to receive answers from Him because they give up and quit trusting Him; they quit using their faith.

I sense that you may be in the midst of a trial right now, and Satan may be tempting you to yield to the pressure of that trial and to stop trusting God and start looking for an easy escape.

Don't do it. Use your faith and wait for God's solution. It will come. While you're waiting read this book; let me show you these things:

- Why your faith is on trial and what the trial means.
- How to be happy about your faith being tried.
- What happens to your faith during a trial.
- What Jesus will do for you in a trial.
- What you can do for yourself during a trial.
- How a trial will teach you patience and what is patience's perfect work.
- How to be victorious in a trial.
- How to turn apparent failure into victory.

George Mueller, one of the faith heroes of the 19th century, said, "The *only* way to learn strong faith is to endure great trials. I have learned my faith by standing firm amid severe testings." So have I. I strongly believe the Lord has anointed me to teach you how to use your faith and how to make sure your faith will withstand any trial. You are about to learn how to have strong faith. You are about to come through your trial victoriously.

Let's Pray

Father, we thank You for Your Word. We thank You that Heaven and earth may pass away but Your Word will endure forever. We thank You, Father, that You watch over Your Word to perform it and to bring it to pass in our lives.

Let Your Word light this reader's path with divine direction and wisdom so that he or she can make quality decisions. Thank You, Father, for Your Word and the Holy Spirit. Jesus, thank You for giving Your life for us. In Your Name we pray.

Amen.

1

Why Is Your Faith on Trial?

The trial of our faith teaches us to take our eyes off ourselves and to walk in Christ's victory.

I do not like trials any more than you do, but a trial will quickly show whether you are willing to walk by faith. It is easy to serve God when you are blessed and things look, feel, and sound good, but it is not easy when everything seems to be against you.

The temptation is to give up and to doubt God's Word. This is when you may feel like asking, "Why is God letting me go through this trial?"

One reason your faith is on trial is because of the cross. Jesus Christ, the Son of God, went to the cross for three reasons:

- To bear the effects, punishments, penalties, and judgment of your sins
- To conquer sin
- To defeat Satan who has the power of sin.

At Calvary, Jesus spoiled the principalities and powers of Satan and made a show of them openly (Colossians 2:15). All that remains is for you to trust God to save and deliver you from your problems.

> For the eyes of the Lord are intently watching all who live good lives, and he gives attention when they cry to him.   Psalm 34:15 (TLB)

Satan lost his power and authority at the cross, but he does not admit it. He certainly does not want you to acknowledge his defeat so he tries everything in his power to defeat *you*. He hates you because God gave you victory there. That's why he gives you problems that not only try your patience, but try your faith in God. However, Jesus said that He has overcome the world.

> ...Here on earth you will have many trials and sorrows; but cheer up, for I have overcome the world.
>   John 16:33 (TLB)

Now this does not mean that you are not going to have any problems in life, but your problems are conquerable as you acknowledge them already conquered at Calvary.

God gave an object lesson about the cross to the children of Israel in the wilderness when they became discouraged and sinned by murmuring and complaining against both Moses and God (Numbers 21).

> "Why have you brought us out of Egypt to die here in the wilderness?" they whined. "There is nothing to eat here, and nothing to drink, and we hate this insipid manna."
>
> Numbers 21:5 (TLB)

In judgment, God sent fiery serpents against them. When they repented, God told Moses to put a brass serpent upon a pole and everybody that looked upon that serpent would be healed (John 3:14-16). This serpent was a type of Jesus Christ bearing our sins on the cross.

The brass symbolized God's judgment upon sin and all the things Satan has put on humanity, such as sickness, discouragement, depression, fear, financial problems, and death (Exodus 27:1-6; Revelation 1:15).

On the cross, Jesus took upon Himself all of humanity's sins and sicknesses and paid God's penalty for them. Through His death He conquered sin and defeated Satan.

> For he hath made him to be sin for us,
> who knew no sin; that we might be
> made the righteousness of God in
> him.   II Corinthians 5:21

> But he was wounded for our trans-
> gressions, he was bruised for our
> iniquities: the chastisement of our
> peace was upon him; and with his
> stripes we are healed.   Isaiah 53:5

Not only did He defeat Satan, but He took
away his power and authority. He went down
into hell (Ephesians 4:8-10), and took the keys
of death and hell out of Satan's hands (Revelation 1:18).

> And having spoiled principalities and
> powers, he made a show of them
> openly, triumphing over them in it.
>   Colossians 2:15

Sin, sickness, and disease have been defeated
and Satan no longer has any authority over
God's children, but he still holds the ancient
enmity against man. He will stop at nothing to
destroy you.

> And I will put enmity between thee
> and the woman, and between thy
> seed and her seed; it shall bruise thy
> head, and thou shalt bruise his heel.
>   Genesis 3:15

Victory over Satan and his power belongs to
every child of God. By accepting Jesus Christ as

your Savior, you accept His victory and place yourself under His protection. Learning to walk in Christ's victory is a vital part of your spiritual growth. The next time Satan tries to make you think he still has power and authority to stop you from believing God's promises, remind him that he was defeated at Calvary. Don't ever give in to the pressures he puts upon you.

Another reason your faith is on trial is because you are doing what is right. Satan gets angry when he sees you doing God's Word, tithing, giving offerings, working in the church, loving your enemies, helping the poor, praying, producing the fruit of the Spirit, and trusting God. He gets so mad that he determines to make you doubt God, so he sends trials against you.

Have you ever known someone who was on fire for God and then troubles and problems came and they got discouraged and quit serving God? The devil got to them. You can't let that happen to you. You have to decide that come hell or high water you are going to stay in faith, be steadfast and unmoved through any fiery trial. You have to decide to trust God no matter how things look or whether anything is working out as you planned. That's the kind of determination it takes to overcome, folks.

The secret is in *deciding* to follow God no matter what. Let me give you an example from the book of Daniel. Babylon's King Nebuchadnezzar attacked Jerusalem and took some of the finest Jewish youth as captives. Among them were Daniel and his friends Shadrach, Meshach, and Abednego.

> Then he [King Nebuchadnezzar] ordered Ashpenaz, who was in charge of his palace personnel, to select some of the Jewish youths brought back as captives—young men of the royal family and nobility of Judah—and to teach them the Chaldean language and literature. ''Pick strong, healthy, good-looking lads,'' he said; ''those who have read widely in many fields, are well informed, alert and sensible, and have enough poise to look good around the palace.''
>
> The king assigned them the best of food and wine from his own kitchen during their three-year training period, planning to make them his counselors when they graduated.
>
> Daniel 1:3-5 (TLB)

Daniel and his friends *made up their minds* that they would not partake of the king's food because it was offered to idols and eating it would dishonor God. They determined to put God first no matter what.

God honored their decision and gave the four of them great ability to learn and they soon mastered all the literature and science of the time. After they passed their oral exams, they were placed on the king's board of advisors and in all matters requiring information and balanced judgment, the king found them to be ten times smarter than his other advisors.

By Daniel's example we have another great truth to observe. You have to watch what kind of spiritual food you eat. To be carnally minded is death; but to be spiritually minded is life and peace (Romans 8:6).

Then the king had a dream which none of his astrologers or magicians could interpret. After Daniel had given the king both the dream and the interpretation, he made him ruler over the whole province of Babylon, as well as chief of all the wise men. Shadrach, Meshach, and Abednego were made Daniel's assistants, to be in charge of all the affairs of the province.

These men consistently did what was right in the eyes of God, for they had made up their minds to do so. About that time, King Nebuchadnezzar made a gold statue, 90 feet high and 9 feet wide, and commanded that all the people worship it. Some jealous officials reported Shadrach, Meshach, and Abednego to the king; other people's words brought problems into their lives.

> There are certain Jews whom thou hast set over the affairs of the province of Babylon, Shadrach, Meshach, and Abednego; these men, O king, have not regarded thee: they serve not thy

gods, nor worship the golden image
which thou hast set up.

Daniel 3:12

In a terrible rage, Nebuchadnezzar sent for
them and demanded to know whether they had
refused to worship the image. ''I'll give you one
more chance,'' he raged, ''but if you refuse, you
will be thrown into a flaming furnace within the
hour. And what god can deliver you out of my
hands then?'' (Daniel 3:15 TLB).

How does a person hold up in the face of
such adversity? Does he trust God or does he
yield to the pressure? Does he do what God says
or murmur against God and quit serving Him?

People like to point the finger at everybody
else, but they should point the finger at the devil
and rebuke him and say, ''Satan, you're not
going to stop me from being a doer of God's
Word. I'm going to be happy because I know the
outcome. I'm going to stay in faith. I'm going
to see the glory of God manifested in my life.''

That's exactly what Shadrach, Meshach, and
Abednego did. They had already decided to follow God no matter what.

Shadrach, Meshach, and Abednego
replied, ''O Nebuchadnezzar, we are
not worried about what will happen
to us.

If we are thrown into the flaming
furnace, our God is able to deliver us;

and he will deliver us out of your
hand, Your Majesty.

But if he doesn't, please understand, sir, that even then we will never
under any circumstance serve your
gods or worship the gold statue you
have erected."

Daniel 3:16-18 (TLB)

They would not bow to the king's gods.
Their faith was on trial in a big way, and all
because they were doing what was right. Would
they bow in the heat of the trial? The king
decided to find out; he ordered the heat to be
turned up seven times. It was so hot that the
men who put them into the fire died from the
blast of heat.

Shadrach, Meshach, and Abednego should
have been cremated quickly, but instead they got
up and walked around. The fire did not burn
their hair or their clothes, and they did not smell
like smoke. When King Nebuchadnezzar looked
into the furnace, he saw not three but four men,
"and the form of the fourth was like the Son of
God" (Daniel 3:25).

Yes, their faith was on trial; it was being tempered by fire. Smoke and fire were all around
them, but they did not become impatient; they
did not quit believing God. They hung in there.
When the trial was over, they were not hurt. The
king, the one who ordered them to be put into
the fire, brought them out and gave them a

promotion; he made them the heads of the whole countryside.

What should you do when you are in a trial? You stick with it. The Bible says he that is patient and overcomes gets the victor's crown; he wins the case.

> To him that overcometh will I grant to
> sit with me in my throne, even as I
> also overcame, and am set down with
> my Father in his throne.
>
> > Revelation 3:21

A third reason your faith is on trial is because Satan accuses those who walk uprightly. That's why he is called the accuser of the brethren (Revelation 12:10). He is like a roaring lion roaming about trying to stop you from serving God (I Peter 5:8).

Satan accused Job of serving God only because he never had any problems and God blessed him continually; but God considered Job to be the finest man on earth, a good man who would have nothing to do with evil.

> And the Lord said unto Satan, Hast
> thou considered my servant Job, that
> there is none like him in the earth, a
> perfect and an upright man, one that
> feareth God, and escheweth [avoided]
> evil?   Job 1:8

Job was constantly examining his heart to see whether he had sinned, and he offered daily

sacrifices for himself, his children and his house-
hold *in case* someone had sinned. Job's
consistent righteousness made Satan angry and
he claimed that if Job were not blessed and protected he would not serve God.

> Hast not thou made an hedge about
> him, and about his house, and about
> all that he hath on every side? thou
> hast blessed the work of his hands,
> and his substance is increased in the
> land.
> But put forth thine hand now, and
> touch all that he hath, and he will
> curse thee to thy face.
>
> Job 1:10,11

God said, "No, Satan, you're wrong. Job
doesn't serve Me just because I am blessing
him." But Satan contended that he did, so God
said, "Okay, find out." Think of this as a court
case: the Righteous Judge, God; Satan, the
accuser; and Job, whose faith was on trial.

The devil, not God, tested Job's faith. God
does not tempt, test, or try a man with evil
(James 1:13-15). Make sure you get this straight:
God did not cause Job's problems.

Jesus said, "In the world ye shall have tribu-
lation [trials]" (John 16:33). I want you to look
at the word "trial" from a different perspective.
A trial is when Satan uses pressures and temptations to get people to stop serving God with
all of their heart, mind and soul. These pressures

can be to do drugs, to get drunk, to do an immoral act, or to doubt. Satan doesn't really care what you do; he just hates your guts and wants you to stop trusting God. He puts all these pressures and temptations on you to defeat you to get you to walk in the flesh as a sinner instead of in the Spirit trusting God, walking in righteousness.

"Why does God let that happen?" you ask. I don't know, but I do know God doesn't cause these pressures, temptations, and trials. If God did not permit the trials, we would not have to face them. But in permitting them, God also provided us with a rescuer; He gave us the Holy Spirit to strengthen us and to give us power to resist temptation and doubt. He gives us faith to overcome. "…and this is the victory that overcometh the world even our faith (I John 5:4)."

When a trial comes it doesn't mean that you don't love God. Job loved God with all his heart. He kept his children in line, and when he *thought* they were sinning, he would fast and pray and offer sacrifices in their behalf.

Nor does being righteous mean that your faith won't be tried. Job's faith was tried because Satan wanted to prove to God that he could make Job sin. Shadrach, Meshach, and Abednego's faith was on trial because Satan wanted to make them bow to the gods of this world.

One of Job's friends came to him and said, "Job, this has happened to you because you've been sinning.''

> For thy mouth uttereth thine iniquity
> [sin], and thou choosest the tongue of
> the crafty.
> Job 15:5
> Your sin prompts your mouth; you
> adopt the tongue of the crafty.
> Job 15:5 (NIV)

''You don't know what you are talking about,'' Job said. ''You are accusing me unjustly. I am a righteous man and I have not sinned.'' (Job 16:17 paraphrased). And he was right; he didn't have a problem with unrighteousness. Unrighteousness will bring problems, but those problems are not a trial of your faith; they are a judgment of your lifestyle. Only repentance will take care of those problems and the sin that caused them.

As I said before, I don't like trials any more than you do, but I know that we are going to have them and sometimes it seems that God is not there. The reality is that He will never leave or forsake us.

> Let your conversation be without
> covetousness; and be content with
> such things as ye have: for he hath
> said, I will never leave thee, nor for-
> sake thee.
> Hebrew 13:5

Don't be one of those people who give up and doubt God is there helping and strengthening you throughout a trial, and beware of

friends and relatives who encourage you to
doubt. Job's wife challenged him, "Are you still
trying to be godly when God has done all this
to you? Curse him and die" (Job 2:9 TLB). But
Job refused to curse God or turn away from serving Him.

> Who am I that I should try to argue
> with Almighty God, or even reason
> with him?
> Even if I were sinless I wouldn't
> say a word. I would only plead for
> mercy.   Job 9:14-15 (TLB)

Instead, he cried from his deep anguish,
"Oh, I *wish* there was a counselor, a mediator,
who would represent me in this trial." From
within our own pressures and trials, we can
relate with Job's cry. But we have a Counselor;
we have a Mediator. Jesus Christ sits at the right
hand of God interceding daily for you and me.

Glory to God! We have a great trial attorney
—Jesus Who bore all penalties of our sins at
Calvary. Now, praise God, we are acquitted,
found not guilty, righteous before God, found
without sin.

When the accuser says we are not healed,
Jesus comes as our Counselor, our Attorney, and
presents the facts. "The facts are, O Judge of the
Universe, God Almighty, this child is healed by
My stripes (I Peter 2:24)."

When the accuser says, "That person is a
good-for-nothing. He used to do drugs and

alcohol, and he is still no good," then Jesus Christ gives the facts. "Almighty Judge of the Universe, this is the fact: This child accepted the sacrifice I made at Calvary and has been cleansed with My Blood and now he is the righteousness of God in Me (II Corinthians 5:21)."

We don't have to go through these trials alone. We have a Counselor, an Advocate; we have One Who is not afraid to face the accuser with the facts, the truth of Calvary.

Job lost everything during his trial, and he could have said, "Well, I've lost it all now. It's over. Why even continue to trust God? Why even continue to look to Him? I've lost the house, my family, the fields, the cattle, the crops...I'm telling you, lightning flashed and burned everything down. There was a whirlwind that tore everything up. It's just been bad, bad, bad, bad."

He could have said that, but he didn't. Job had a bulldog-like tenacity and an attitude of total confidence in God. "Though God slay me," he said, "yet will I trust Him (Job 13:15)." In other words, I will never stop trusting God even to the grave. Job had made up his mind that no matter what happened, even if he lost his own life, he was not going to deny God.

You must make sure that you have that same attitude, for when the battle comes you are going to need it. You are the one who decides when the battle is over. It's not over until it's over and that's when the total manifestation of victory comes.

The fourth reason your faith is on trial is because God is testing your faith. God does not test us with sin, but He does test us to see if we will be obedient to His will. Satan tests us with disobedience. God tests us to be doers of His Word and not hearers only.

At times God will test your heart to see whether it is fixed on Him (Psalm 112:7). You see, faith works by love (Galatians 5:6) and love casts out fear (I John 4:18). Only when you truly love can you release your faith and have what you say. But you only love by being vitally united with Jesus Christ and by drawing your very life from Him (John 15:4). Unless you abide in Him, keep His commandments and walk in His love, you will not bear the fruits of the Spirit, one of which is faith (Galatians 5:22-23).

God tested Abraham's love and faith by asking him to sacrifice his only son, Isaac, to Him (Genesis 22:1-13). Abraham passed this test of obedience because his heart was not afraid to trust God; his heart was fixed upon God's love and faithfulness to him.

Elijah demonstrated a mighty faith by challenging 450 false prophets and calling down fire from heaven. When the people of Israel refused to repent, he commanded the heavens to hold the rain for three and one half years.

God miraculously provided for Elijah during the drought. While the rest of the countryside was suffering, Elijah was camped by the brook Cherith, enjoying plenty of water and food that God sent him by ravens. But one day the brook dried up and Elijah faced the toughest test of his faith.

The brook did not dry up because Elijah missed God, but because other people missed God. The drought would not have been necessary if the people had repented and served God. But God chose to use this situation to test Elijah's faith. He told him to go to a poor widow who was starving to death and ask her for food and water. That was a big test of faith and obedience.

Elijah and I have shared this same test of faith. The devil said to me, "Tilton, you're out there taking money from poor people." You can look at God's instructions in the natural, or you can look at them through the eyes of God. I choose to always look at God's instructions through His eyes. God told Elijah, and me, to go to people who were outcast, hurting, and dying and to prophesy to them that God would meet their needs if they would believe and act upon God's instructions and give out of their need.

The widow had one small pancake-sized piece of bread for herself and her son, and Elijah asked for it. Can you imagine that? Elijah's faith was definitely on trial. How could a strong man take from a widow and an orphan? The widow's faith was on trial. How could she give her son's only food to a strange prophet?

I believe the Spirit of God went before Elijah and prepared the widow's heart to trust God through the prophet. When she gave the cake to Elijah, they both passed God's test of obedience. Throughout the drought, they had plenty to eat—all their needs were met.

When you let Jesus Christ come into your life, He will come and sup with you (Revelation 3:20). If He's going to eat with you, that means you are going to have something to eat too.

God said, ''Prove Me. Let me have your money, and I will supply your needs. Trust Me to be your God and to care for you.'' (Malachi 3:10-12 paraphrased). Do you have enough faith to tithe, to give God ten per cent of your gross income? That's a test from God. That's not a bad test because God doesn't test with evil. He tests with good. He will tell you what He will do if you will believe and trust Him. He said, ''If ye be willing and obedient, ye shall eat the good of the land (Isaiah 1:19).''

God wants to know if you have put Him first in your life, and if you will trust Him, no matter what comes your way.

These trials are only to test your faith, to see whether or not it is strong and pure. It is being tested as fire tests gold and purifies it—and your faith is far more precious to God than mere gold; so if your faith remains strong after being tried in the test tube of fiery

> trials, it will bring you much praise
> and glory and honor on the day of his
> return.   1 Peter 1:7 (TLB)

God values your faith, so He purifies it, even
as gold is purified by fire, for He knows the true
qualities of faith. Like gold, faith has beauty, softness, resistance to corruption, and strength.

When God becomes the focus of your faith,
it draws forth a lovely, soft glow to your coun-
tenance. Peace overrules pain. Confidence
controls the crisis. Hope conquers despair. In the
midst of a storm there is peace when you enter
in the rest of faith. It's like the eye of a hurri-
cane where there is calm and peace in the center.

Faith's softness makes you easy to work
with; it allows God to shape you into any form
He desires. It is utterly confident that God will
perform His Word.

Faith's resistance to corruption keeps you
from Satan's evil influences and keeps your life
from being tarnished. It destroys the appeal of
the temptations Satan places before you for it
sees them through the eyes of God.

Faith depends on the Word of God for its
strength. The more of the Word that is added
to your faith, the stronger it becomes, and you
have power to wield the sword of the Spirit like
an expert warrior.

I have had a lot of experience with trials, and
I still do not like them. But I have learned to
stand firm on God's Word through each one and

to be happy when things are rough because
when my faith has passed the test, it always
comes out stronger. When the storm is over, the
Righteous Judge will find that I was obedient to
God's Word, resisted the temptations of Satan
to give up, and stayed in faith victorious giving
glory to God. Nothing is impossible with faith
and patience.

When your faith is on trial it means that:

- You are righteous
  Psalm 34:17-19

- God is still with you
  II Corinthians 1:3-4
  Isaiah 43:2-5
  Romans 8:37-39

- You *have* faith
  I Peter 5:7-10

- You are overcoming
  I Peter 5:10-11
  II Corinthians 4:8-10, 15-18

- God values your faith
  1 Peter 1:7

- Your patience has a chance to grow
  James 1:2-4

2

Why Should You Be Happy When Your Faith Is Tried?

When your faith is sorely tried, count it all joy because God is giving your faith a chance to grow.

The book of James was written to Jewish Christians who were being persecuted and whose faith was being severely tried because of their love for Jesus Christ.

> Dear brothers, is your life full of difficulties and temptations? Then be *happy*, for when the way is rough, your patience has a chance to grow. So let it grow, and don't try to squirm out

of your problems. For when your
patience is finally in full bloom, then
you will be ready for anything, strong
in character, full and complete.

James 1:2-4 (TLB)

James took special care to show them that the
deciding factor in whether they overcame their
trials was their attitude. He said it is important
to be encouraged, happy, and joyful when you
face difficulties so that you can bring about the
fulfillment of God's promises in your life.

The trial of your faith specifically calls for
dependence on God and patience to purify and
strengthen your faith, but the rewards of such
a faith, according to Peter, are praise, glory and
honor.

**The trial of your faith keeps you dependent
on God.** Dependence is a natural consequence
of trust; and, of course, trust is based on perfect love which casts out all fear (I John 4:18).
You can only be dependent when you recognize
God as your sole Source. Dependence walks by
faith, not by sight, and to overcome trials you
must continue walking by faith—the faith that
comes from the Word of God (listening to God).

The only way the devil can defeat us is by
keeping us from listening to the Word of God,
or if we have heard it, by stealing it from us. He
keeps chipping away at one promise after
another, trying to make us doubt whether God
ever keeps His Word. If he can do this, he destroys our faith.

Jesus told us to be of good cheer because He has overcome all the problems of life (John 16:33). That does not mean you won't have to face any problems; it simply means He conquered them all at Calvary.

If you are saved and have made Jesus Christ Lord of your life and the Greater One is living inside you, then you can depend upon God's power and strength to overcome Satan's attacks. You can depend on His faithfulness to perform His Word (Jeremiah 1:12; Matthew 5:18).

God said, "Be happy." He never told you to run around and be sad. Make a decision that no matter what is going on, no matter what difficulties are in your life, you are going to be happy for the joy of the Lord is your strength (Nehemiah 8:10).

"Bob," you say, "you have never faced what I have had to face." Maybe not, but I do know that it would not make any difference to me; I would still be happy because God commanded me to be.

"But, Bob, you just do not know what I am facing." No, and I know that there is always an opportunity to become discouraged, but I also know that Jesus has overcome the world. He has given me the victory.

> ...In the world ye shall have tribulation: but be of good cheer; I have overcome the world.
>
> John 16:33

> But thanks be to God, which giveth
> us the victory through our Lord Jesus
> Christ.   I Corinthians 15:57

I know that Jesus wants me to get excited, be
encouraged and be happy because He has won.
I have the Overcomer inside me. Why should
I be unhappy?

The only reason I have to be unhappy is if
I have done wrong:

- If I have yielded to temptations.
- If I have slid back into doubt and
  unbelief.
- If I have yielded to pressures and am
  doing exactly what Satan wants me
  to do.
- If I have started looking at the problem instead of looking at Jesus for
  the solution.
- If I am concentrating on the difficulties instead of the victories.

God has promised to help me and His Word is
sure. He never fails. He is faithful to perform His
Word.

I believe this is a powerful truth on how to
handle life's difficulties. I don't believe James is
saying that you should lie down, roll over, and
play dead when there is a problem or difficulty.
Instead, you should stand your ground and exercise your faith in the promises of God's Word.
You should be patient and steadfast; you should
not be moved off course by the pressures of the

trial. You should be happy because God will give you victory.

Jesus is the solution to each trial and difficulty you face. His very name means *salvation, deliverance, and solution.* He will help you overcome every trial. Don't doubt God's Word or yield to the pressures of your trial. Don't look at the problem; look to Jesus. Be happy and rejoice that He is your God.

> A merry heart doeth good like a medicine: but a broken spirit drieth the bones.   Proverbs 17:22

If you will focus all your attention on Jesus Christ and His victory, you will have an underlying peace that will let you be happy in spite of your circumstances. Don't be sad and discouraged and try to squirm out of your problems. Be happy and face them with total confidence that Jesus is giving you victory over them. You can depend on Him to deliver you.

When your faith is being tried, it teaches you patience. "Patience" means *bearing pain or trials calmly*. Exercising patience does not mean you let problems run over you; rather, it means handling them scripturally, correctly, and calmly. It means waiting calmly for the answer because you know God controls the situation. In other words, you don't let the problem get the best of you. You bear the pain or the trial calmly in victory, knowing that the victory is God's. You don't get anxious, upset and frustrated before you see the answer.

Many Christians miss it right there. When they don't see an instant solution, they get upset; they squirm; they blame God; and they give up too soon. Some go from one failure to the next because they never learn to handle a trial calmly without complaining.

That's what happened to the children of Israel in the desert. Things weren't going the way they wanted them to go, so they murmured and complained—constantly. Sure they had some problems, but they also had God watching over them and guiding them. He gave them fire to warm them at night and a cloud to protect them from the heat of the day. Every time they needed food, God sent it. Always He rained down manna from Heaven; at times He sent in the quail. When they needed water, He squeezed it out of the rocks.

But sometimes things didn't go the way they wanted them to and the Israelites were quick to say, "God's left us. He doesn't care." They stopped believing and started complaining, talking doubt and unbelief. They whispered their dissatisfactions; they blamed God for every bad situation; they bellyached; they criticized; they spoke negatively about everything; they doubted God's ability to keep them.

There was one time I was going over some major things God had asked me to do. Frankly, I began to doubt and question myself about whether I had heard it from God. One night I lay awake going over the problem in my mind when suddenly, God spoke clearly to my heart, "Why do you doubt Me? Why do you feel I cannot keep you in the cleft of My hand? Why do you doubt I can direct your steps? Am I not big enough to do it?"

Immediately I prayed, "God, forgive me." In a few seconds of time God showed me that the steps of a righteous person are ordered of God. I saw beyond the pressures of the trials to the bigness of the love of God and His ability to direct my steps—even when I don't know or cannot see that He is directing them.

That's why it is so important to walk patiently by faith and not allow Satan to defeat you. You have to believe that God is directing your steps, that He is keeping you and directing you whether it looks like it or not. You cannot doubt that He is guiding you and caring for you.

When your faith is sorely tried and it looks like nothing is going right, be encouraged, be happy, count it all joy and be patient. Continue to do God's Word and to walk forward. Believe that God is with you, for He is! You *can* believe it!

Some of you do not like to be patient. That's why you lose the victory—you don't give God time to work out your difficulties. Or you don't give God time to bring you a complete victory, healing, prosperity, peace, joy, etc. Sometimes God delivers *out of* a problem; at other times He delivers *through* a problem. The secret to

winning is waiting for God's timing and that
requires patience, and you can learn patience
only by going through the hard places.

**Trials test your faith to see whether it is
strong and pure.**

> These trials are only to test your faith,
> to see whether or not it is strong and
> pure. It is being tested as fire tests gold
> and purifies it—and your faith is far
> more precious to God than mere gold;
> so if your faith remains strong after
> being tried in the test tube of fiery
> trials, it will bring you much praise
> and glory and honor on the day of his
> return.   I Peter 1:7 (TLB)

> Dear friends, don't be bewildered or
> surprised when you go through the
> fiery trials ahead, for this is no strange,
> unusual thing that is going to happen
> to you.
>
> Instead, be really glad—because
> these trials will make you partners
> with Christ in his suffering, and after-
> wards you will have the wonderful joy
> of sharing his glory in that coming day
> when it will be displayed.
>   I Peter 4:12-13 (TLB)

Faith deals with the supernatural. It is the
gift God gave you to bring the unseen into reality and to make the impossible possible, but it

only grows during storms. When the storm is the fiercest and the conflicts the sharpest, that is when your faith grows. That's its most productive soil; that's when it bears the most fruit.

The strongest tree does not grow in the forest but out in the open where the winds twist it, bend it, and beat upon it until it becomes a giant. Then its wood is valuable. In the same way, a man of faith grows through hardships, buffetings, trials and triumphs; he grows best when the hot blasts of hell almost blow him off his feet, when he is forced to stand on the Word of God against all odds, and when he learns he is more than a conqueror in Jesus Christ.

Exercising faith in the face of danger makes us stronger and better. An example is the story of a seafood wholesaler on the east coast who was losing money shipping cod out to the west coast. Each time, the shipment was turned down because the fish arrived with a mushy texture. He tried shipping it in salt water. Then he packed it in ice. Nothing worked.

Then he tried something outrageous. He shipped the live cod in a tank of water which also contained ocean catfish, the cod's natural enemy. The cod arrived on the west coast with a fine, firm texture and the wholesaler began to profit. (Don't you imagine those cod had a busy workout avoiding the enemy?)

Facing down our enemy Satan can keep us in good spiritual shape. Resisting the devil gives our spiritual muscles a good workout, and we grow strong and firm in faith. That is why as Christians we can rejoice when our faith is under attack. Because <u>we know that we have victory in Christ, we can only be better for the trial.</u>

3

What Happens to Your Faith During a Trial?

Every time your faith is tried, it comes out strengthened. God will always bring you through victoriously, if you trust Him.

When your faith is being tried and it looks like everything is against you, be encouraged. Things are happening to your faith but you need not worry; your sole responsibility is to continue to do the Word of God and trust Him.

Peter said your faith is purified by fire in order to bring out its true qualities (I Peter 1:7). Like gold, faith has beauty, softness, resistance to corruption, and strength.

Gold is warmly beautiful and it retains its beauty forever. Faith is like that; the more it is used, the more beautiful it becomes. Faith casts a warm glow over the person who is using it and warms all those nearby.

Gold is adaptable to shaping. It can be melted without harm; it can be hammered into thin leaves. It can be used to cover other objects for beauty and protection. Faith that is centered in the Person of Jesus Christ is also malleable; it takes no thought of its own wishes, but desires only to please God and to bring glory to Him.

Gold is highly prized because it is enduring; it never rusts or dissolves away. Strong acid alone will not affect it. Only a mixture of concentrated nitric and hydrochloric acids will dissolve it. It is the only metal fire cannot harm. In fact, each time it goes into the fire it comes out better and more refined than before. So it is with faith that focuses on Jesus Christ. It resists corruption. Fiery trials only refine and purify it.

Gold can be easily alloyed with other metals to increase its strength while retaining its beauty. The most effective alloy for faith is the Word of God. Not only does the Word strengthen faith, but it energizes and perfects it, causing the beauty of Christ to shine through the individual.

Finally, gold is valued because of its scarcity. Gold is mentioned in the second chapter of Genesis and in the next to the last chapter of Revelation, and hundreds of times between. It has been used to make practically everything imaginable, yet it is scarce. So too is true faith. A lot of people talk about faith, use faith formulas, and work on their faith, but *true* faith is scarce. Perhaps that is why God allows our faith to be tested; He is developing within us a precious treasure. I don't believe God sends problems and trials but I do believe He definitely brings a positive out of a negative when we keep our eyes on Him.

The trial purifies your faith by revealing any flaws. There are three major flaws which make faith imperfect: impatience, bad attitudes, and doubt and unbelief.

Several years ago God told me, "Many people fail to receive from Me because they become impatient during trials and quit believing My Word and trusting Me to give them the victory." These people get upset and let pressures from the trial get the best of them if they don't get immediate answers; then they give up and quit trusting God. Impatience defeats faith.

If you really want to win, it is important that you believe God is directing your steps whether it looks like it or not. That's called walking by faith. Many times God puts a thought or a decision into your mind and you are not aware of it until later. I read in Psalms where God opens up our minds in the night and tells us what we need to know.

> I will bless the Lord who counsels me,
> he gives me wisdom in the night. He
> tells me what to do.
>
> Psalm 16:7 (TLB)

God will not always instantly deliver you out of your trial, but He will always bring you through it. Job had to go through his trial, but despite the circumstances he did not give up or turn away from God. Instead, he remained patient, steadfast, and unmovable.

Job did not understand why his friends were judging him so harshly, or why God was allowing him to be tried, but he knew he could depend upon the faithfulness of God so he waited patiently for God's deliverance.

Patience is a very important factor. To be patient is to be *steadfast, unmovable, and always the same*.

> But they that wait upon the Lord shall
> renew their strength; they shall mount
> up with wings as eagles; they shall
> run, and not be weary; and they shall
> walk, and not faint.
>
> Isaiah 40:31

"Wait" in Hebrew is *qavah* and it *implies firmness and constancy of mind, to expect anything, and to wait steadily and patiently till it is effected*. "Patience" in Greek is *hupomone* which means *to abide under control*. Patience, then, is staying under God's control. It is not letting difficulties, pressures, or the enemy keep you from being Spirit-filled and Spirit-led.

Impatience, then, is losing control. Have you ever noticed when a trial or pressure comes that many tend to binge on foods as a way of handling the pressure? Is that losing control? Or maybe you want to return to former bad habits?

Before you were born again, you did things you knew you shouldn't do because you didn't have the strength to resist, and you were ashamed. Satan wants to drag you back into that old nature, so he tries to drag up all the old garbage. We are all subject to temptation; all of us will slip back if we don't stand fast, stay patient and abide under the control of the Lord.

God said that those who wait patiently upon the Lord will renew their strength (Isaiah 40:31). In other words, as you wait patiently for God's deliverance, your expectations of hope will come to pass.

Besides impatience, giving up, throwing in the towel in disgust, stomping out of the church in the heat of anger, and coming against those who try to teach you the Bible and how to live by faith will all make you lose. Bad attitudes will defeat your faith.

You must stay in faith no matter how hot the fire gets. Even when it looks like you have failed and all others have given up, you must stand upon the Word of God.

Job could have bad-mouthed God, but instead he said, "Though God slay me, yet will I trust him." He had a my-God-can-do-anything and I'm-going-to-trust-Him attitude. He was willing to put his life on the line if need be.

Some folks say, "Well, if a problem comes, I'm not going to serve God." Had Shadrach, Meshach, and Abednego felt like that, they would have missed walking with the Son of God! Their attitude rings across the centuries: "Our God is able to deliver us; and he will deliver us out of your hand, Your Majesty. But if he doesn't, please understand, sir, that even then we will never under any circumstance serve your gods or worship the gold statue you have erected" (Daniel 3:17-18 TLB).

Some people can't see God for seeing the man; their attitude is, "Who does he think he is? He's just a man." Jairus, one of the synagogue rulers, came and asked Jesus to come lay His hands on his little daughter and heal her. As Jesus was going, an unknown woman with a desperate need shoved her way through the crowd to touch his clothes (Mark 5:22-29). She did not know Jesus is God; she knew only that He had healed others and she needed healing so badly. Her attitude whispered, "If I may but touch His clothes, I shall be whole."

Not long ago a woman was watching me on television. She was extremely ill with a heart condition, arthritis, allergies, bleeding ulcers, and a problem with her colon. As she watched, I turned to the camera and said, "God has healed you; now get out of that bed." She didn't know me and she could have said, "Who does he think he is?" But she didn't. Instead, she got out of bed and was healed from that moment. She didn't hear Robert Tilton; she heard Jesus.

If you will keep your attitudes right and be open to the Spirit of God, you will hear Jesus in each of your trials. Your attitude needs to be the same as the Apostle Paul's: "I am not ashamed of the gospel of Christ: for it is the power of God unto salvation to every one that believeth" (Romans 1:16).

The Gospel *is* the power of God. Jesus *is* the power of God unto salvation for everyone that believes. It is *now the power of God*, the healing of God, the seeding of God, the forgiving of God, and the multiplying of God. Whatever you give Him, He blesses and gives back to you multiplied.

But doubt and unbelief will destroy your faith; it is a major flaw. While Jesus was en route to Jairus' house, a person came and said, "Don't bother getting Jesus to come to your house because your daughter is already dead. It's too late. He can't do anything now." (Mark 5:35 paraphrased).

Unbelieving friends will talk you right out of your faith. Jairus was already using his faith to get his daughter healed. He was praying, believing, acting. Then his friends tried to steal his faith. If you are going to get your answer to prayer, you must learn how to deal with doubt and unbelief wherever you find it.

As soon as Jesus heard the word that was spoken, he saith unto the ruler of the synagogue, Be not afraid, only believe.

And he suffered no man to follow him, save Peter, and James, and John the brother of James.

And he cometh to the house of the ruler of the synagogue and seeth the tumult [turmoil], and them that wept and wailed greatly.

And when he was come in, he saith unto them, Why make ye this ado, and weep? the damsel is not dead, but sleepeth.

And they laughed him to scorn. But WHEN HE HAD PUT THEM ALL OUT, he taketh the father and the mother of the damsel, and them that were with him, and entereth in where the damsel was lying.

And he took the damsel by the hand, and said unto her, Talitha cumi; which is, being interpreted, Damsel, I say unto thee, arise.

And straightway the damsel arose, and walked; for she was of the age of twelve years. And they were astonished with a great astonishment.

And he charged them straitly [immediately] that no man should know it; and commanded that something should be given her to eat.

Mark 5:36-43

Jesus dealt with doubt and unbelief by first removing the doubters from His presence. After He had raised the little girl from the dead He told her parents not to tell anyone about the miracle. Do you think that was because He didn't want anyone to know about Him? No, He didn't want Jairus and his wife talking to their friends who didn't have any faith. He did not want people planting doubt and unbelief in their hearts. Don't hang around anybody that doesn't believe or you'll get their plague.

Jesus always separated Himself from doubt and unbelief before He went to pray. Once He had to take a blind man outside of town to heal him. He frequently withdrew to the mountains to pray and to be alone in God's presence.

If you really want to win, you too will have to separate yourself. There is a price to pay for the presence of God in your life. There must be a separation from unbelievers and the distractions of life so you can hear His still, small voice.

When God has answered your prayers, be careful who you tell. The natural inclination is to tell all your friends the good news immediately. However, if they are filled with doubt and unbelief, they are not able to receive your news and they will kill your faith. Usually they do this real religiously; they wait for a vulnerable moment when the devil has already been attacking you with doubt, then quietly, they jab their little knives of doubt into your faith until it is dead.

> Give not that which is holy unto the dogs, neither cast ye your pearls before swine, lest they trample them under their feet, and turn again and rend you.   Matthew 7:6

Another way to deal with doubt and unbelief is by avoiding counterfeit Christians. Jesus called them tares; He said they looked like wheat, smelled like wheat, and acted like wheat, but they were not genuine (Matthew 13:24-30). They are a bunch of hypocrites. You can usually recognize them because they whisper against the teaching and the preaching of the church. They suggest that the church is not preaching the whole Gospel. They are not interested in living the Gospel themselves; they merely want to plant doubt.

Another way to deal with doubt and unbelief is to avoid traditionalists who preach that God no longer performs miracles. These people generally look at the Bible from a human viewpoint; they preach the Word of God without acknowledging its power. These people have a form of godliness, but they deny its power

(II Timothy 3:5). This kind of preaching makes the Word of God non-effective in your life and destroys your faith.

Another way to deal with doubt and unbelief is to displace negative thoughts with the Word of God. Every time you doubt, read the Word. Memorize the Word and continually rehearse it in your thoughts. Overcome every doubt with the Word of God.

We have people who write us and make vows to God and then they start believing the lies of the devil instead of what God says in the Bible. They forfeit their miracle every time. Jonah said, "They that observe lying vanities forsake their own mercy" (Jonah 2:8). The devil lies three dimensionally: in your thoughts, in your heart, in your feelings. You have to realize that he is a liar and not listen to him.

The most powerful way to overcome doubt and unbelief is to concentrate on Who God is. When you become obsessed with *knowing* God, your faith will take hold and banish every negative thought from your being.

The trial strengthens your faith. This is done by letting your patience grow. Those who possess this virtue are unafraid, full of hope, confidence and courage. They are, according to James, ready for anything.

The trial perfects your faith. When your faith is perfect, every grace that is present in Christ should be shown in your life. That means you should be producing the fruit of the Spirit in abundance.

Every time your faith goes into the fire it comes out strengthened, with fewer flaws, and closer to perfect. When hard times come, you must remember it is your faith on trial—not you. Your sole responsibility is to stand fast on the Word of God and to trust Him.

4

What Will Jesus Do for You in a Trial?

Jesus conquered Satan at Calvary, and He has given you authority over the trials he brings your way.

God promised you victory, not a life without problems. He will either deliver you from the problems or walk with you through them. His protection is always total and complete within His plan to bring your faith to maturity. If from your perspective it seems that God is not protecting you, it is because you do not see the whole picture.

Jesus promised never to leave you. There will be periods when you will not feel God's

presence, but this does not mean that you have
sinned or that He has left you. God is watching
to see if your faith is strong enough so that you
can stand on His Word and wait patiently for His
answer.

> And they that know thy name will put
> their trust in thee: for thou, Lord, hast
> not forsaken them that seek thee.
>
> Psalm 9:10

There are different ways of looking at protection. You can look at it as God not letting
anything ever happen to you, or you can realize that God is inside you and that He gives you
the power to overcome every problem.

Job lived before Christ's victory over Satan
and God did not dwell *in* man at that time, but
God protected man from the outside, like a shep-
herd looking after his flock. Before his trial, Job
was totally protected by God this way and he
did not have any problems. But God allowed
Satan to take Job's material possessions, his
family, and his health in order to prove to Satan
that Job's faith was strong, pure, and genuine.
God did not tell Job what was happening; He
trusted Job's faith to pass the test.

Because of Calvary, God now dwells within
you. He has made you righteous and has given
you power over Satan. Where Job had external
protection and was safe, you have both external
and internal protection. Jesus is with you all the
time. You are constantly under His watchful protection.

...I will never leave thee, nor forsake thee.   Hebrews 13:5

At that day ye shall know that I am in my Father, and ye in me, and I in you.   John 14:20

And he that keepeth his command- ments dwelleth in him, and he in him. And hereby we know that he abideth in us, by the Spirit which he hath given us.   I John 3:24

Jesus rebukes the trials that you face. There will be times when God, through His mercy, will step in and defeat the devil for you. At other times, He expects you to claim the victory He has already given you.

I have heard people say, ''I just cannot quit smoking. I wish God would deliver me from these cigarettes.'' God has already delivered you! When Jesus defeated Satan at Calvary, He broke all of Satan's power over God's children and that includes bad habits. All you need to do is stop. By continuing to smoke, you are yielding to Satan's temptation. If you will resist, you will find you have the power to overcome it.

Jesus and His disciples were crossing the Sea of Galilee when a fierce storm arose (Mark 4:35-41). The boisterous waves broke into the boat and threatened their lives while Jesus was asleep in the back. Peter and the others got all upset and began to shake Jesus to awaken Him, ''Wake up,

Jesus, how can you sleep when we are all going to drown?"

Jesus rose immediately and rebuked the storm; then He turned to them and asked, "Where is your faith?" Even though Jesus was asleep when the storm came, He wanted them to know that He was still there with them and would respond to their cries for help. He is always ready to rebuke the storms in your life. He also expects you to use your faith and rebuke the storms.

Also, Jesus gives you power and dominion over Satan. Because Job only had God *with* him, he needed someone to be his counselor, to represent him and plead his case (Job 16:21). But your Counselor is Jesus Christ Who lives *in* you (Ephesians 6:10 TLB). Jesus has made you a new creature; your sins have been washed away; and now you are the righteousness of God in Christ.

> Therefore if any man be in Christ, he is a new creature: old things are passed away; behold, all things are become new.
>
> For he hath made him [Jesus Christ] to be sin for us, who knew no sin; that we might be made the righteousness of God in him.
>
> II Corinthians 5:17,21
>
> For if by one man's offence death reigned by one; much more they which receive abundance of grace and

of the gift of righteousness shall reign
in life by one, Jesus Christ.

Romans 5:17

Therefore, unrighteousness has no authority and
dominion over you. The devil has no place in
your life. Now you reign in life; you have
authority and dominion over everything in the
earth, including any deadly thing that would
harm you.

He that believeth and is baptized shall
be saved; but he that believeth not
shall be damned.

And these signs shall follow them
that believe; In my name shall they
cast out devils; they shall speak with
new tongues;

They shall take up serpents; and
if they drink any deadly thing, it shall
not hurt them; they shall lay hands on
the sick, and they shall recover.

Mark 16:16-18

And God blessed them, and God said
unto them, Be fruitful, and multiply,
and replenish the earth, and subdue
it: and have dominion over the fish of
the sea, and over the fowl of the air,
and over every living thing that
moveth upon the earth.

Genesis 1:28

The heaven, even the heavens, are the
Lord's: but the earth hath he given to

the children of men.

Psalm 115:16

And the seventy returned again with joy, saying, Lord, even the devils are subject unto us through thy name.

And he said unto them...Behold, I give unto you power to tread on serpents and scorpions, and over all the power of the enemy: and nothing shall by any means hurt you.

Luke 10:17-19

Jesus defeated the devil and gave you victory, but you have to walk in it—even in difficult times. If you don't, you will lose.

God has also given you a spiritual armor for protection:

- Helmet of salvation so that you can renew your mind.
- Breastplate of righteousness so that you can walk uprightly before Him.
- Truth with which to gird your loins.
- Shoes in which to walk by faith and not by sight.
- Shield of faith to quench every fiery dart that Satan sends toward you.
- Sword of the Spirit, the Word of God, to defeat every enemy and every difficulty you face.

(Ephesians 6:13-17)

Jesus has given you the keys of the kingdom. He wants you to learn how to resist the devil yourself.

> Verily I say unto you, Whatsoever ye
> shall bind on earth shall be bound in
> heaven: and whatsoever ye shall loose
> on earth shall be loosed in heaven.
>
> Matthew 18:18

When I had the actual face-to-face encounter with Satan not long ago, I saw myself using five keys to defeat him.

- Be clean and righteous
- Use the authority of the Name of Jesus
- Have faith in the Name of Jesus
- Bind Satan
- Tell the devil what to do, and speak the Word of God only

Life is not fun and games. We are in a warfare. It is a matter of life and death that you learn to use these keys. Make sure that you are not slothful; don't let the devil catch you unprepared.

Satan is a defeated foe. Jesus defeated him first at Calvary; I have defeated him and you can defeat him by the blood of the Lamb and the word of your testimony. Don't be afraid; you have authority in the Name of Jesus. Use it continually.

Jesus rebukes your lack of faith. After Jesus rebuked the storm for Peter and the disciples,

He asked, ''Where was your faith?'' Jesus wanted them to learn to use their own faith. You see, faith *in* God brings the faith *of* God.

Jesus taught that God is absolutely faithful to keep His promises and is therefore worthy of trust, that He is steadfastly loyal in His love toward us, and that He never changes. Because He knew His Father's character so well, Jesus had utter confidence in Him and submitted in loving obedience to His will. That's what He wants you to do. When you do, you will come to know God better than ever and your faith will soar.

Jesus makes you an overcomer. Satan wants to get you back; that's why he keeps trying your faith. Anybody can serve God as long as everything is going great, but a little problem will quickly reveal what you are made of. If you let difficulties keep you from trusting God, you will lose your reward.

You cannot lie down when a trial comes; you have to continue to walk by faith and wait upon the Lord. The Bible promises that those who wait on Him shall renew their strength and mount up with wings as eagles (Isaiah 40:31).

Don't give up. Be happy! Count it all joy when you face trials, for if you stay in faith and wait with patience, you will overcome. If you live by faith and not by sight, you will be victorious. Jesus said in Revelation 3:21 that the person who overcomes will be allowed to sit with Him on

His throne. The overcomer also wears the crown of life.

> Happy is the man who doesn't give in and do wrong when he is tempted, for afterwards he will get as his reward the crown of life that God has promised those who love him.
>
> James 1:12 (TLB)

Therefore, no matter what type of fiery trials come do not give in to them. Stay in faith, have patience, and be steadfast; continue to trust in the Lord and He will make you an overcomer.

5

What Can You Do for Yourself During a Trial?

When you trust in God and act on His Word, you release a faith that not only moves mountains, but moves the heart of God.

In ancient times when a king ran short of money, he would lay siege to a neighboring country and place its cities under tribute. This meant, in effect, that he increased his revenue by collecting the taxes from those cities. That's what King Sennacherib of Assyria did to Judah.

When King Hezekiah learned of Sennacherib's plans, he called a war council and instructed the people to plug the springs and cut off the water outside the city walls. Then they repaired the walls, added to the fortifications, built a second wall around the first, reinforced the fort, and made more weapons and shields.

When Hezekiah addressed his army, with its new recruits and newly appointed officers, he said, ''Be strong, be brave, and do not be afraid of the king of Assyria or his mighty army, for there is someone with us who is far greater than he is! He has a great army, but they are all mere men, while we have the Lord our God to fight our battles for us!'' (II Chronicles 32:7 TLB).

Sennacherib, using the ever powerful fear tactics, taunted the citizens.

- He's trying to get you to commit suicide by staying there.
- He destroyed all your favorite gods, now you're stuck with his.
- I've never lost a battle.
- No god has been able to stop me.
- What makes you think your God can do any better?

With these familiar threats ringing in their ears, Hezekiah and Isaiah, the prophet of God, cried out in prayer for God's help, and God sent *one* angel who destroyed the entire Assyrian army with all its officers and generals!

After Assyria's defeat, Hezekiah's prestige and respect soared; tons of gifts arrived from the surrounding nations. Hezekiah was a hero. About that time, he became deathly ill and prayed for healing, and God gave him a miracle. But he didn't respond with true thanksgiving and praise because he had become proud. Only after he humbled himself and repented, did he prosper in everything he did.

"However, when ambassadors arrived from Babylon to find out about the miracle of his being healed, God left him to himself in order to test him and to see what he was really like" (II Chronicles 32:31 TLB).

Sometimes God wants to see what you can do for yourself, so He watches to see how you respond to a test. God doesn't leave us but sometimes He is very quiet to see what we do with our faith in Him. Make sure that you don't waste the time He gives you. Aside from continuing to praise God and to thank Him for His blessings, there are four major things you can do to help yourself during a trial.

You can use your own faith. You can remove your problems when you have faith in God— utter confidence in God and total submission to His will in your life. If you believe and act upon God's Word, without doubt, you release a faith that not only moves mountains, but that moves the heart of God for He wants nothing more than to have His children to absolutely trust Him to keep His promises.

> And Jesus answering saith unto them,
> Have faith in God [in the Greek, liter-
> ally, *have the faith of God*].

For verily I say unto you, That whosoever shall say unto this mountain, Be thou removed, and be thou cast into the sea; and shall not doubt in his heart, but shall believe that those things which he saith shall come to pass; he shall have whatsoever he saith. Mark 11:22-23

You can take authority over the situation. How? By deciding to believe God's Word, to obey it, and to be joyful in the midst of the trial.

If ye be willing and obedient, ye shall eat the good of the land.

Isaiah 1:19

The joy of the Lord is your strength.
Nehemiah 8:10

Offer unto God thanksgiving; and pay thy vows unto the most High;

And call upon me in the day of trouble: I will deliver thee, and thou shalt glorify me. Psalm 50:14-15

Delight thyself also in the Lord; and he shall give thee the desire of thine heart.

Commit thy way unto the Lord; trust also in him; and he shall bring it to pass. Psalm 37:4-5

Be happy because you are about to see the glory and the delivering power of God manifested. The answer is not going to come in your strength, but in God's. When you get excited about Him, you take authority over the problem in His name. You are no longer operating from fear, but from love and faith.

- If you don't have enough money to pay your bills, get excited because you're about to see God pay them.
- If you don't know what to do, get excited because God is giving you wisdom.
- If you don't have enough strength to perform your tasks, get excited because you're about to experience the strength of God.

Don't forget that God is big enough to direct your steps, inspire your thoughts, give you bread to eat and water to drink. Take God's Word and believe it; you will get exactly what you believe for.

You can rebuke the devil. Satan has attacked me with just about every trial imaginable, but every day I fight back with the Word of God. I read it; I memorize it; I say it over and over to myself; I meditate on it; I put it into practice in my life. I continue to trust God even if it looks like nothing is coming to pass. I am determined to trust God and His Word. Sometimes I get to the place where I cannot listen to anyone except God's Word.

The best way to rebuke Satan is with the Word of God. That's what Jesus did. That's what I do, and that's what you'll have to do if you want to be an overcomer. Live close to the Word and use it as your weapon, for God never fails to perform it.

You can call for God's help. He is always attentive to the cry of His children. When Peter cried, ''Don't you care that we are drowning?'' Jesus immediately arose and rebuked the storm. When the three Hebrew children were thrown into the furnace, He came down and walked with them. When Daniel was thrown to the hungry lions, God closed their mouths. When Jonah cried out to Him about the heat, He caused a vine to grow quickly and shade him.

In other words, our God is able to deliver us and He will. All you have to do is cry out to Him.

6

How Does the Trial of
Your Faith Teach Patience?

*Patience is the key to victory during trials.
God wants us to learn to abide under
His control and trust His timing.*

A trial comes and the pressure gets up—
it gets heated; it gets hot. That's when
some people quit. Others want to quit,
but instead they keep trusting God and standing on His Word and before long they overcome.
The difference between losing and winning is
patience.

Patience is the key to your victory. You can't
give up and win. Despite the portrayal of modern life on television, most things in life do not

happen instantly. There is a trend in our country toward acceleration; we are urged to do things
faster, and faster, and faster. We want instant
results. Sometimes this leads us to expect
immediate results spiritually, but God operates
on His own time schedule.

> For ye have need of patience, that,
> after ye have done the will of God, ye
> might receive the promise.
>
> Hebrews 10:36

Patience makes you seek God. When you
need answers, you go to where the answers are.
That's why you need to search the Bible and ask
God about your circumstances. If you want to
know what to do, ask God. When you ask for
wisdom, believe that you have it.

> If you want to know what God wants
> you to do, ask him, and he will gladly
> tell you, for he is always ready to give
> a bountiful supply of wisdom to all
> who ask him; he will not resent it.
>
> But let you ask him, be sure that
> you really expect him to tell you, for
> a doubtful mind will be as unsettled
> as a wave of the sea that is driven and
> tossed by the wind; and every deci-
> sion you then make will be uncertain,
> as you turn first this way, and then
> that. If you don't ask with faith, don't
> expect the Lord to give you any solid
> answer.   James 1:5-8 (TLB)

Then as you make your decisions, believe that God is inspiring your thoughts and giving you divine direction. If the God you serve cannot keep and guide you, then you need not serve Him. But He can, He will, and He does! It is your responsibility to stay in faith. Don't let impatience rob you of your victory.

Find the will of God; then do it. Continue to do His Word until you see the promise fulfilled in your life. Despite the pressures, do the will of God. Despite the trials, do the will of God.

God does not lie. If He said He would do something, He *will* do it. Marte and I have discovered this to be absolutely true. But we have also learned that we have to seek His face continually. Whatever God said will come to pass, but we have to believe that we receive it.

Patience makes you wait for God's answer. God knows that if He were to always give us answers instantly, we would soon look at Him as being no more than a genie in a magic lamp. He wants us to learn to abide under His control and to allow Him to direct our steps. He wants us to abide in Jesus and in His Word. He said if we would do that we could ask anything and it would come to pass.

> If ye abide in me, and my words abide in you, ye shall ask what ye will, and it shall be done unto you.
>
> John 15:7

Many people forfeit their faith and their
answers by becoming impatient. Over and over
in the Scriptures, God warns that impatience will
destroy your faith.

> Don't be impatient. Wait for the Lord
> and he will come and save you [He
> will rescue you]! Be brave, stout-
> hearted and courageous. Yes, wait and
> he will help you.
>   Psalm 27:14 (TLB)

> In your patience possess ye your souls.
>   Luke 21:19

> For if you stand firm, you will win
> your souls.   Luke 21:19 (TLB)

> Rest in the Lord, and wait patiently for
> him: fret not thyself because of him
> who prospereth in his way, because of
> the man who bringeth wicked devices
> to pass.   Psalm 37:7

Isaiah said those who wait patiently upon the
Lord will renew their strength (Isaiah 40:31). That
sounds like getting your second wind to me, like
lengthening your endurance. In other words,
when you stand fast on God's Word and
patiently do it, you will eventually see your
expectations come to pass.

Patience makes you steadfast. Despite
opposition, you are unmoved. Despite accusa-
tions, you are unruffled. Despite Satan's attacks,
you are unafraid. You can only be steadfast when

you know beyond any doubt that God Almighty is your champion and that you truly have nothing to fear.

When you are steadfast, difficulties mean nothing to you for you know Someone Who has never failed to overcome any difficulty. You can't give up and win. God wants you to know this so He allows you to wait for His answers. But they *will* come for He has promised you victory.

Patience makes you victorious over every trial. So be happy and stop complaining and trying to squirm out of your problems; let your patience grow and mature.

> Dear brothers, is your life full of
> difficulties and temptations? Then be
> happy, for when the way is rough,
> your patience has a chance to grow.
> James 1:2-3 (TLB)

Recently my parents and I were picking up their airline tickets at the airport. Ahead of us, three senior citizens were having a problem getting their luggage checked in. I watched a woman directly behind them start squirming and then complaining to the people around her about the problems the senior citizens were having.

Meanwhile, the line next to us opened so I moved into that line. This woman also saw the new line open, but she was so busy complaining that she failed to get into it. As a matter of fact, as we were leaving she was still standing there complaining.

Complaining is a form of impatience. Satan uses it to make you lose control during a trial. You see, he will try to bring your òld man back to life to influence you to do and say things you know are not right. This makes it doubly important that you submit to God when your faith is being sorely tried and nothing seems to be going the way it should.

Difficulties will come and your faith will be tried, but if you give God time to work out the problem you will receive a complete answer. The Bible is full of great men and women of God who were patient and stayed true to God even though they suffered greatly. After each trial came victory.

> Take, my brethren, the prophets, who
> have spoken in the name of the Lord,
> for an example of suffering affliction,
> and of patience.
>
> Behold, we count them happy
> which endure.   James 5:10-11

Job lost everything but continued to trust God. After the trial he was abundantly blessed (Job 42:10).

Though they faced a blazing furnace, Shadrach, Meshach, and Abednego staunchly stood on their belief that God would deliver them (Daniel 3:17-30). Then, all three were made ministers in the province of Babylon. Daniel rested in the lions' den and God delivered him.

Joseph was so sure of deliverance that he made his sons promise to carry his bones out of Egypt when they left. For 120 years, Noah worked on a boat in anticipation of rain which no one had ever seen. Abraham waited 25 years for the birth of his son and then put him on the altar to sacrifice him to God, knowing that God had promised to make him a great nation through Isaac.

Elijah watched the brook dwindle week after week; first it became a thread, then shallow pools, then dry, cracked mud. Finally, even the ravens quit coming. Only then did God speak, "Arise, get thee to Zarephath."

Victory after victory. How many more do I need to name? The Bible is full of people who learned patience through the trial of their faith, yet they did not doubt God. Patience is your key to victory. Dig into the Word of God and trust Him to perform His Word; He will—in His time.

Only the trying of your faith makes patience grow. "Why do we need patience?" you may ask. Because when patience gets to do her thing in your life, you will be perfect; you will lack nothing. That's what God wants for you—for you to lack nothing.

Patience makes you ready for anything. When you learn to exercise patience, you allow God to bring about the fulfillment of His promises in your life. You can handle anything that comes your way calmly and scripturally. You don't get upset, frustrated, or anxious. You go to God's Word and find the answer; then you wait for Him to fulfill His Word. It's that simple. Patience makes you expect that God will always bring you the victory. It gives God time to work things out.

Patience makes you strong in character. Patience keeps you from becoming a weak-kneed coward. It gives you courage to face your problems immediately and to trust God to help you make the right decisions. It takes away fear because patience is based on faith which is grounded in love. It keeps you from being moved by difficulties. It keeps your eyes on Jesus Christ; it keeps you expecting Him to answer your prayers.

Patience makes you full and complete. You become the person God designed you to be. You respond to His Word, operating in and using the gifts He has given you. You become an overcomer—not of just one trial, but continuously.

So don't ever give up. Stay in the Word of God. Be happy! Count it all joy when you face hardships for your patience is growing and your faith is being perfected.

7

How Can You Be Victorious in a Trial?

God gives us specific steps to follow in the road to victory. Obedience to His Word will show us the way.

It is the failure to do God's Word—not the storms—that will destroy you. What happens is that you, like the house in the Lord's parable, will collapse before the storms if you have no foundation (Matthew 7:24-27). In this chapter, I want to show you how to build your foundation for life so that you can always withstand the storms.

The first step is to study the Word of God. A recent survey, conducted by the Barna

Research Group of Glendale, California, showed that only 25 per cent of all born-again Christians read the Bible every day. That means that 75 per cent of them are building their lives on the sand and they are collapsing before every storm. No wonder we have so many casualties!

Jesus said that the wise man hears His instructions and follows them. Yet, you cannot do God's Word until you know what He says. Your faith comes from hearing the Word of God (Romans 10:17).

Even though you think you do not understand it, you need to store God's Word in your subconscious mind against the day of trouble. This makes it available for recall when the Holy Spirit needs to comfort, direct, or teach you during a time of difficulty.

> Thy word have I hid in mine heart, that I might not sin against thee.
>
> Psalm 119:11

> Thy word is a lamp unto my feet, and a light unto my path.
>
> Psalm 119:105

> But he [Jesus] answered and said, It is written, Man shall not live by bread alone, but by every word that proceedeth out of the mouth of God.
>
> Matthew 4:4

> Study to shew thyself approved unto God, a workman that needeth not to

be ashamed, rightly dividing the word
of truth.   II Timothy 2:15

Reading devotional and instructional books, listening to teaching tapes or Christian radio, and attending Bible study groups are wonderful tools for your spiritual growth, but they cannot take the place of your reading the Word of God daily.

For years now, Marte and I have made it a practice to read the Bible through once a year, and I encourage the members of my church and my staff to read God's Word daily. I hope you will too because without God's Word, you have no foundation to build upon.

The second step is to do God's Word. From time to time, we all are pressured to stop believing God's Word. Whenever you receive a revelation or an encouragement from the Word, Satan tries to hinder your feeding off it or drawing strength from it because he knows he is doomed to defeat if you do God's Word, for God always performs His Word.

God is not a man, that he should lie; neither the son of man, that he should repent; hath he said, and shall he not do it? or hath he spoken, and shall he not make it good?
                              Numbers 23:19

Jesus says the wise man does God's sayings. If you have been reading the Word, you know what God says. His command is simple: Just do what He said.

- If you're facing a trial, be happy.
- If you're merry, sing.
- If you're afflicted, pray.
- If you're sick, call for the church elders and let them pray.
- If you've sinned, repent.
- If you need wisdom, ask God.
- If you don't know how to pray, let the Holy Spirit pray through you.
- If someone makes you go one mile, go two.
- If someone offends you, forgive him.

Find out what God says about your circumstances and do it—no matter what anyone else says or how things look. Just do God's Word, and keep on doing it until you have the victory. Trust God even if it looks like nothing is working. God will perform His Word (Jeremiah 1:12). Faith is believing and asserting what God says.

Step three is to develop a prayer life. Recent studies show that children who talk frequently with their parents have fewer drug problems, fewer social adjustment problems, are less rebellious, and are rarely involved in crime. If this happens in human family life, how much more important it is that we talk with our Heavenly Father.

That's what prayer is—just listening and talking to your Father. The enemy does not want children talking to their Father; he wants them to mistrust and rebel. Prayer helps you abide under the control of Jesus Christ; it helps you continue to do God's Word; it helps you trust God; it gives you power to stand against Satan's attacks.

The fourth step is to put on the whole armor of God. God does not send you out to face Satan alone or unprotected. He goes before you and protects you from behind (Isaiah 52:12). He provides you with protective armor.

> Last of all I want to remind you that your strength must come from the Lord's mighty power within you.
>
> Put on all of God's armor so that you will be able to stand safe against all strategies and tricks of Satan.
>
> For we are not fighting against people made of flesh and blood, but against persons without bodies—the evil rulers of the unseen world, those mighty satanic beings and great evil princes of darkness who rule this world; and against huge numbers of wicked spirits in the spirit world.
>
> So use every piece of God's armor to resist the enemy whenever he attacks, and when it is all over, you will still be standing up.
>
> But to do this, you will need the strong belt of truth and the breastplate of God's approval.

> Wear shoes that are able to speed
> you on as you preach the Good News
> of peace with God.
>
> In every battle you will need faith
> as your shield to stop the fiery arrows
> aimed at you by Satan.
>
> And you will need the helmet of
> salvation and the sword of the
> Spirit—which is the Word of God.
>
> Pray all the time. Ask God for any-
> thing in line with the Holy Spirit's
> wishes. Plead with him, reminding
> him of your needs, and keep praying
> earnestly for all Christians every-
> where.   Ephesians 6:10-18 (TLB)

It is up to you to put on and use the armor God
had provided. You need it all in every battle;
don't neglect it.

Step five is to walk in faith. How can Jesus
accomplish anything great in your life when He
has to constantly drag you out of the water to
keep you from drowning? Peter asked to walk
to Jesus on the water, and he was doing fine until
he started looking at the boisterous waves. That's
when Jesus had to rescue him (Matthew
14:28-31).

When Peter started looking at and perceiv-
ing the things around him, he began to walk by
sight. He got his eyes off the Lord and the word
the Lord originally gave him. Walking by sight
always deteriorates your faith; it causes you first

to doubt and then to sink. The faith of God would have continued to work in Peter's life had he kept walking. Peter, like you and me, had to learn the secret is to always focus on Jesus Christ.

Satan doesn't let people walk on the water without endeavoring to stop them. You might as well realize that every time you step out to follow God's Word a storm will arise to test your faith.

The next step is to be filled with the Spirit. God gives you His Holy Spirit to help you resist discouragement, unbelief, and doubt, and to strengthen your weaknesses.

> Likewise the Spirit also helpeth our infirmities: for we know not what we should pray for as we ought: but the Spirit itself maketh intercession for us with groaning which cannot be uttered.
>
> And he that searcheth the hearts knoweth what is the mind of the Spirit, because he maketh intercession for the saints according to the will of God.   Romans 8:26-27

There are times when you won't know how to pray because you don't have the Bible memorized, or you don't understand what you have read. In those times, the Holy Spirit will intercede for you. He will search your heart and put what He discovers there together with the mind of Christ and offer it to God.

The Holy Spirit knows the situations in your life. He knows what is going on in the spirit-world; He knows which demons are attacking you and what battles you are facing. He prays the perfect will of God for and through you. He is your Comforter; He is present to encourage and strengthen you.

That's why it is important to be filled with the Spirit. Praying in tongues is like getting a drink of Holy Spirit water to strengthen you. That's why it is important to pray—both with understanding and in the Spirit. When you do, you are strengthened, you begin to get ideas and wisdom, and He helps you make decisions.

> But the Comforter, which is the Holy Ghost, whom the Father will send in my name, he shall teach you all things, and bring all things to your remembrance, whatsoever I have said unto you.   John 14:26

> But ye shall receive power, after that the Holy Ghost is come upon you: and ye shall be witnesses unto me both in Jerusalem, and in all Judaea, and in Samaria, and unto the uttermost part of the earth.   Acts 1:8

> Rejoice evermore.

> Pray without ceasing.

> In every thing give thanks: for this

is the will of God in Christ Jesus concerning you.

Quench not the Spirit.

I Thessalonians 5:16-19

Pray at all times—on every occasion, in every season—in the Spirit, with all [manner of] prayer and entreaty. To that end keep alert and watch with strong purpose and perseverance, interceding in behalf of all the saints [God's consecrated people].

Ephesians 6:18 (AMP)

Next, utilize all that God has given you. See yourself as an heir of God and joint-heir with Jesus Christ now. See yourself with creativity, wisdom, inspired ideas, and divine direction. See yourself with more than enough in Jesus Christ; see yourself as complete and sufficient in Him. You are in Jesus and there is no lack in Him. Since Jesus is inside you, there is no lack in you. There is no one smarter than you because you have the mind of Christ. Close your eyes and see every favor and earthly blessing abounding toward you in Jesus Christ.

Anytime the devil hits you with inferiority, fears, discouragement, or distress close your eyes and see yourself standing in the presence of God, with God loading you down with blessings. See yourself having authority over every power of the enemy. See yourself blessed because you have been redeemed from the curse

of the law and Abraham's blessings are yours
(Galatians 3:13-14).

**The next step is to associate with those of
like faith.** If you hang around doubt and
unbelief that is exactly what you will get. You
need to choose your friends carefully; deliber-
ately look for those who truly believe God's
Word and do it.

There was a man in the Bible who was paralyzed and confined to his bed (Mark 2:1-5).
When Jesus came to town, his friends tried to
take the man to Him so that he could be healed,
but the crowds were so large that they couldn't
get near Jesus. Instead of slinking off in discouragement, they took the roof off the building
and lowered the man, cot and all, through the
crowd. When Jesus saw their faith, He told the
man, "You're healed." Evidently the man
believed it, because he got up, picked up his bed
and walked out. You need friends like these—
friends whose faith is visible.

**The last step for being victorious in a trial
is to worship God through giving.** Giving is a
way of demonstrating to God that you believe
that He is and that He rewards those who dili-
gently seek Him (Hebrews 11:6). Giving can also
be a way of disciplining yourself to keep God
first in your life and to seek Him above all else.

Furthermore, giving is a public testimony of
your faith and dependence on God. It is a decla-
ration before this world and before Satan and all

his demons that you are under the protection and anointing of God.

> Thou has caused men to ride over our heads; we went through fire and through water: but thou broughtest us out into a <u>wealthy place.</u> I will go into thy house with burnt offerings: I will pay thee my vows, which my lips have uttered, and my mouth hath spoken, when I was in trouble.
>
> Psalm 66:12-14

> Vow, and pay unto the Lord your God: let all that be round about him bring presents unto him that ought to be feared.   Psalm 76:11

Thus when your faith is on trial you will be victorious if you consistently:

- Study God's Word
- Do God's Word
- Develop a prayer life
- Put on the whole armor of God
- Walk in faith
- Be filled with the Holy Spirit
- Utilize all that God has given you
- Associate with those of like faith
- Worship God through giving

Therefore bring forth fruits meet for repentance.

Matthew 3:8

8

When Is the Apparent Failure of Your Faith Victory?

Look beyond appearances when you see failures—it may be success in disguise.

God sees things differently from the way we do. While we observe outward appearances, God sees the heart (I Samuel 16:7). Remember, the Red Sea hid the road of deliverance from the children of Israel as well as from Pharoah. What Satan used for bad—fear of drowning in the sea—God used on him and Pharoah's army. So what looked like failure at first was really a victory for God.

Sometimes we are too quick to criticize and

to blame others for stepping out of faith because they have a difficulty. Some of the heroes of faith listed in Hebrews 11 died with their faith switch still on. Does it mean they were in doubt and unbelief because they died without seeing the fulfillment of their faith? No! I guarantee that on the other side they received their answers. They simply went into Heaven overcoming. God had something better.

I am not a faith preacher who condemns people because it looks outwardly that their faith has failed. I believe that if we love God and are walking in all the knowledge we have, and if we have not doubted the promises of God, we are victorious no matter how it looks. Remember, we live by faith not by sight.

God sometimes chooses to use apparent failure to change your direction. The brook dried up for Elijah. Are we going to say that Elijah missed God because the brook dried up? No. The brook dried up because the people of Israel missed God. God rescued Elijah and sent him to the next place where he was going to feed him miraculously. God had something else, something better for him. Abundantly above all we can ask or think.

Elijah passed the test of obedience at Cherith, and God chose to use the drying up of the brook as an opportunity to move Elijah to a bigger test of obedience. He had not told Elijah, but God was strengthening Elijah's faith so that he could face 450 false prophets and call down fire from heaven. Do you call that failure?

God considered Job to be the finest man on earth (Job 1:8 TLB). Yet he removed the hedge and allowed Satan to test Job's faith and take everything material from him.

But after the trial, God told Job's three friends that He was angry with them because they had not spoken right about Him as Job had. He told them to make a burnt offering for their sins, get Job to pray for them, and He would spare them.

When Job prayed for his friends, God restored his wealth and happiness twice over. Do you call *that* failure?

Do you call it failure to get to walk with the Son of God in a fiery furnace? And to come out with nothing burned but your bonds? And then be made ministers?

When you pass God's test, you have not failed—no matter what man thinks. "Faith is the confident assurance that something we want is going to happen. It is the certainty that what we hope for is waiting for us, even though we cannot see it up ahead" (Hebrews 11:1 TLB).

Every person listed in this chapter had tests and triumphs, failures and successes, disappointments and fulfillments—yet they never doubted God's promises. That's why God had them listed as heroes of faith. The strength of faith is believing God's Word and doing it—

always, without giving up.

Yes, there are trials and our faith is tried by Satan to get us to be disobedient to God. But on the other side, God watches as a judge, sitting on His bench hearing and watching for evidence (our actions) that we have been obedient to His word (laws). Pass God's test and let Him turn a trial into a victory of faith. Be patient for in due season you will reap if you faint not (Galatians 6:9). "I love you. I will never leave you helpless," saith the Lord.

9

How Others Overcame

God delivers those who stay in faith and remain patient, steadfast, and unmovable throughout their trials.

We all have problems and trials at one time or another in life, and many times are tempted to fall into doubt and unbelief, forgetting God's promises.

When faced by such trials, it is easy to slip back into our old nature if we do not abide under God's control. Therefore, don't quit when a trial comes, but walk by faith and wait upon the Lord expectantly, steadfastly, and patiently.

We have studied in this book the stories of saints of old who remained firm through the

fiery trials of their faith. But now I want to
encourage you with the testimonies of some
modern day saints who have discovered that
God is still the same—and what He did for the
believers of the Old and New Testament, He will
do for us today!

Leslie and Pat had decided to have children
right away when they got married. But
four years passed, and Pat still had not
conceived. They went to the doctor and took
several tests, but there was nothing physically
wrong with them. They should have been able
to have children, however Pat was still unable
to conceive. Frustrated, she grew tired of fight-
ing and gave up. She had lost all hope.

Leslie and Pat were monthly supporters of
this ministry, and were seeding toward a $1,000
vow. One day, Leslie gave Pat a prayer cloth that
I had prayed over. She followed my instructions
and wore it on her body for about a month. Then
Pat lost the prayer cloth, but she was at peace
because she knew she had been obedient. Now
it was up to God.

Two months after Pat lost her prayer cloth,
she found out that she was pregnant. Now she
and Leslie have a healthy baby boy! "We know
our baby is a gift from God." says Pat. "God
used the prayer cloth to stretch my faith into a
new area. To get my mind off myself and onto
the power of God."

Their faith passed the test and God blessed their home.

Virginia's whole world had fallen apart two months before she moved in with her older son. He desperately needed a car, and she needed finances for her younger son's school tuition. She only had a one dollar bill and $7 in pennies when she discovered my program, but she still decided to release her faith by making a $1,000 vow of faith in God.

Virginia sowed her seed and prayed, but her situation grew worse. She stayed in faith, but it seemed the more she prayed, the worse things got. "In between praying, I kept telling the children the Lord was going to bless us. I had made a vow and the Lord would honor it in His time. They thought I was crazy!" she writes.

However, Virginia's faith was not in vain. A few months later, she was notified that she had inherited $17,000 from an aunt she had met just once, and that was over 30 years ago! God answered Virginia's prayers. Her older son got his car, and her younger son got a chance to return to school. Now she is seeding toward a $5,000 vow.

"There had been a problem locating me when the estate was settled in 1986...it had been there for me all the time. When I released my faith by making a vow, God released my blessing! My children watched me pay off my 'impossible' vow, so they don't criticize quite as much as they used to. Praise God!" writes Virginia.

Even when her loved ones doubted, Virginia stood firm all through the trial of her faith.

Gerry was an unemployed private duty nurse. Her husband was a truck driver, and since she could not find a nursing position, she co-drove an 18-wheeler with him. Then one day he walked out, leaving her with four children to support, bad credit, and no place to live.

Gerry did not know what to do. She looked for a nursing job but found no openings that would meet her family's needs. Finally, she put her children in foster care and went back on the road, driving an 18-wheeler cross-country to make ends meet.

This situation lasted two years, and Gerry could see no way to change it. Satan robbed her of every penny she made. She did not even have a home. When she came off the road she had to stay with her mother or with the family that cared for her children. She was at the end of her rope.

Gerry was staying with her mother when she discovered my program, and her life changed dramatically after she began releasing her faith through vowing. She made a $500 vow for unsaved loved ones and began sowing her seed. Soon I gave a word of knowledge that ministered to Gerry, and she made a $1,500 vow, believing God for a solution to her problems. That Christmas, Gerry had rented a motel room so she and her children could spend some quality time alone, but she decreed that next Christmas was going to be different.

After making her vow, Gerry took a step of faith and quit her truck driving job. She began scanning the papers for a nursing position, and the first number she called turned out to be a wonderful job that God used as a channel of blessing.

Gerry's father gave her enough money for a one-bedroom apartment, but what she really wanted was a mobile home. Five months after she began sowing her seed, Gerry got the three-bedroom mobile home she had asked for, but God did not stop there. He also provided her with some property in the country so that her children could have a place to play, and she would not have to worry about paying rent on trailer space.

Gerry was definitely blessed with answers. Not only did she get a good job and a home for her children, but her brother accepted Christ as his Savior, and she received a brand-new car! She also received physical and emotional healing. Gerry was rescued from a place of desperation, and now she dwells in a place of peace and fulfillment. Faith and patience in the midst of a trial brought victory.

"As I make vows, I am putting all my trust in God and his ability to take care of me," says Gerry.

Foster and Cathy needed $700,000, and they needed it quick. They had spent two frustrating years trying to turn Foster's dream into a reality, and now it seemed as though all their time, energy and money would be lost.

Foster's dream was an inspired idea that could help save the lives of countless children. He and Cathy wanted to manufacture a doll that had a tape recorder inside. The messages it played would teach children how to avoid strangers and how to react during emergencies. But when they went to a toy manufacturing plant in Hong Kong, they discovered the project would take nearly one million dollars.

Foster and Cathy sold their home and used the equity to finance their business. They made several trips to Hong Kong, Korea and many other countries in their search for investors. They met men of great wealth and stature, but nothing materialized. It seemed that Foster's dream had come to an end, but still they refused to give up.

Foster and Cathy were down to their last $1,700 when they turned on my television program. They listened as I gave a word of knowledge which described their situation perfectly. "There's a businessman watching, and your business keeps hitting brick walls. You have charisma and the ability to sell, but there are strongholds that need to be broken. You need to make a $1,000 vow to break the strongholds!''

Foster was skeptical and didn't respond, but he couldn't forget what I had said. It was all true. He was known for his charisma and ability to sell, and his business was coming up against brick walls. Cathy felt God was telling them to make a vow for deliverance, and she prayed that her husband would realize that God was talking to them.

About a week later, Foster was watching as I interviewed a business couple, people that he could identify with. I gave another word of knowledge for the businessman who still hadn't made a vow, and one of my guests pointed a finger at the camera and said, ''What are you waiting for? Make that vow!''

After a confirming word from Cathy, Foster released his faith by making a $1,000 vow, believing for God to break the bondage off their business and provide them with a large investor. Three days later, Foster and Cathy received a phone call from a wealthy man interested in their product. Immediately, they sowed $100 toward their vow, and within ten days, the man agreed to invest the $700,000 they needed!

Foster and Cathy are rejoicing over all the great things the Lord is doing in their lives. They know that making and paying toward their vow is what changed their entire situation. They put their faith on the line; they put it on trial and won their case. "Vowing released me from doing it my way," says Foster. "I gave it all to God."

Katie loved the Lord and paid her tithes, but she failed to see the blessings of God in her life. She was tired of government housing, food stamps, and unemployment, but it seemed there was no way out.

Katie heard about my daily television program from her sister, and she decided to tune in. As she listened to my teaching, Katie realized that she could do something to change her circumstances, and she released her faith by making a $100 vow. Soon afterwards, she received an unexpected gift of $2,000!

Katie's first vow was just to get some faith seeds in the ground. Later, she made a $1,000 vow for miracle money. After Katie began paying toward her vows, the Lord provided her with a job. Katie was given favor, and within one year, she received two raises and a vacation in Orlando with a free hotel room and $189 in spending money thrown in.

As a child, Katie had always dreamed of owning a mobile home, but she never thought it could happen. Shortly after getting her job, Katie's dream came true. She not only received her mobile home, but it was set up on a rent-free lot!

Katie felt the Lord urging her to get off all government programs because He was her source of supply. Now, Katie is overjoyed because when she goes grocery shopping she can pay the cashier with her own money instead of food stamps. Even her children have been blessed since she began vowing. God has provided four of them with housing and transportation. Katie not only won her case in the trial of faith, her life changed from lack to abundance. "Since I started vowing and paying my vows, God has blessed me," writes Katie. "Thank you so much for your prayers."

Roxie and Robert were losing their battle against financial burdens. Robert was injured on the job five years ago, and he had not worked since. His disability checks only provided a meager $86 a week, and he felt inadequate as a husband and provider. Roxie cleaned homes, but arthritis in her hands limited the amount of work she could do.

The constant financial pressure was beginning to affect Roxie and Robert's marriage. Their home was in turmoil, and embarrassing weekly visits from bill collectors and the sheriff's department added to the tension. They lacked transportation because their vehicles were broken, and they could not afford to have them repaired. Their gas had been disconnected. Their electricity was next.

Roxie made and seeded toward a $50 vow. Then one day she was listening to my daily television program while working in the kitchen. I gave a word of knowledge for someone whose home was in turmoil, and Roxie knew that I was speaking to her. She responded by making a $1,000 vow for Robert to find a good paying job that did not require manual labor.

In spite of their bad credit, Roxie and Robert were soon blessed with a new van. This not only gave them a means of transportation, but it also provided a way for Robert to make a living. God brought along a man who showed him that he could make money by using the van to transport workers to their place of employment. During his first week of driving, Robert netted $100 each day!

Roxie was watching my program again when I told people who needed healing to lay their hands on the television screen. Roxie obeyed, and shortly afterwards, the pain and swelling in her hands disappeared! Now her housecleaning business is booming, and she is planning to hire extra help.

Since Roxie and Robert began sowing their seed, they are making almost six times as much as they used to. Peace has been restored to their home, and there is no danger of foreclosure. The embarrassing visits from creditors and the sheriff's department have ceased because all their bills are current.

Roxie continually praises God because of the miracles He performed through vowing. "You sparked a flame in me that was dormant." she says. "No one has ever inspired my faith like you."

Roxie's faith soared through her trial and came out strong. This kind of strength worries the devil and he goes on the offensive as he did with Brenda.

B renda had released her faith by making and seeding toward a $500 vow. Several months later, Satan launched a vicious attack against her family. One day, just a few minutes after Brenda had checked on her two sons, a shot rang out, followed by a shriek. She prayed as she made her way toward the bedroom, and when she opened the door, she discovered that her four year-old son Todd had accidentally shot himself in the head with a .22-caliber pistol.

Brenda held Todd and prayed aloud as her husband rushed them to the hospital. She thanked God in advance for His blessings and for blessing them as a family. She rebuked Satan and placed the entire situation in God's hands. "I told Todd that Jesus loved him," writes Brenda. "He said, 'I know, Mama, I love Jesus too.' " Brenda was filled with an inner peace and assurance that everything would be all right.

At the hospital, the doctors found that the bullet had lodged against Todd's skull. They did not expect him to survive, but Brenda knew that God had everything under control. Todd spent two and a half weeks in intensive care before being moved to a private room. After five weeks, he was released from the hospital.

Brenda and her husband did not have insurance, and after three weeks Todd's hospital bill had escalated to over $51,000. Brenda stood in faith, and the hospital took care of the bill for them! Someone also set up two trust funds to pay any additional medical expenses.

Brenda continued to claim healing for her son and watched as his condition continued to improve. Now, Todd is walking, talking, and singing songs of praise. "Jesus is healing my little boy more and more each day," writes Brenda. "He truly blesses those who put their faith in Him and His Word."

When Satan attacks your children, it's a sign he's desperate to destroy your faith. But Brenda set her face like a flint and came through her trial victorious.

10

Overcome by Vowing and Giving

When your faith is on trial, learn to strengthen it by vowing and giving. That will keep your faith from being crippled.

When we are going through a trial of faith, the pressures and tribulations clamor for our attention, and sometimes we tend to take our eyes off God and focus our faith in other directions. Often we do not even notice that we are doing it. In spite of our sincerest efforts to be centered in God, we may be actually concentrating our faith in what we need to get out of the trial!

What we are doing is taking our faith off its rightful Object and placing it in temporal things that have limited value. In other words, our faith gets misplaced and that kind of faith is as good as no faith at all. So instead of growing through the trial, our faith may actually become crippled.

If you are not careful your faith can also suffocate in another kind of trial: the worries and stresses of day-to-day living. You have bills to pay, a family to provide and care for, and a hundred other things that claim your attention. So, you get caught up in these cares and then start looking at God as a kind of cosmic vending machine, an insurance policy in a time of trial.

The trouble with that kind of thinking is that it impairs your faith. Because it does not consider the character and nature of God as the Lover of His creatures, it diminishes your ability to love Him. It impairs your fellowship and weakens your communion with your Creator and Provider, the very Author of your faith.

Like the paralyzed man at the pool of Bethesda (John 5:1-10), you are so concerned with your trial, your dire circumstance, and the burden of your human weakness that you forget God your Helper. When you keep looking at your problems and how you think they ought to be solved, you end up closing yourself off from Jehovah-Jirah, your only Provider, and His perfect solution.

Jesus asked the man, "Do you want to be healed?" The man's attention was so focused on his helplessness that he did not realize Who stood before him. His answer was a complaint against his circumstance and an excuse for his powerlessness: "I have no one to take me to the water..." His narrow, palsied faith kept him from seeing the only One able to restore him to wholeness.

When you look at your trials and dwell on the obstacles that render you powerless, you are in effect telling God that He has to first overcome these obstacles in order to answer your prayers. So, you limit God's ability to bless you when you confess those restrictions. The paralyzed man was telling Jesus, "I can't get well because I can't get into the water when it's troubled—that's the only way I can be healed—and nobody will help me."

To be effective and vibrant, your faith has to be centered and focused in the character and faithfulness of God to such a degree that being delivered from your trial takes second place in importance. You need to desire the Giver above the gift, the Creator above anything He created, the Deliverer above the deliverance.

This desire must be expressed from the heart. Your first desire must be to know Him, hear Him, and obey Him without questioning, trusting always in His goodness and His will for your perfect good.

Amazingly, against all human reasoning, that very attitude of seeking God first will result in "all these [good] things [being] added unto you." When your priorities are in order, your faith is active, and your hope is placed on the right Object, your deliverance will come supernaturally according to God's *perfect* will and timing.

But how can you reach that level of faith? How can you grow in it? How can you find that liberating truth? You must seek it in the Word of God, studying how Jesus dealt with those He met who had needs in their lives. Study His questions and listen to His answers. He did not ask the man, "Do you want me to help you get in the pool?" He went to the heart of the matter when He asked, "Do you *want* to be healed?"

When Jesus healed the man with the withered hand (Luke 6:6-10), He asked him to stand in the middle of the synagogue and stretch out his hand. The Lord was asking him to reach beyond his natural ability and resources. When the man forgot his trying circumstances, stopped concentrating on his limitations, and focused on Jesus, his very act of trust, faith and obedience brought him deliverance.

In the same way, in I Kings 17, the widow's act of faith, giving out of her need and trusting in the word of the prophet, supplied her and her son's needs, as well as the prophet's. She looked beyond herself and her trials, and trusted God speaking to her through the prophet.

Vowing and worshipping God through your giving to God's work is one of the best ways to stretch your faith during a trial—but only when your vow goes beyond your natural resources or abilities. I do not need much faith to vow $100 if I have $2,000 in a savings account; but if I do not even have a savings account and can barely pay my bills, then a $100 vow will stretch my faith indeed. For I will have to seek God to supply the seed to pay that vow—and that will take my eyes off my trials and focus them on God instead.

That is probably the greatest benefit of vowing. It changes my focus and causes me to believe God in a measure beyond my natural ability. Marte and I are always in the process of making a vow or paying a vow because we know that this action keeps our attention focused on God and protects us from being entangled in the worries, cares, attractions, distractions and trials of this world.

Vowing protects us from the natural tendency to place our faith and confidence in our job, possessions, financial security—in other words, our own resources. Vowing keeps us from misplacing our faith because it forces us to focus on Jesus. It liberates us from fear and worry when our faith is being tried, and keeps it vital. It is unimpaired by a self-centered focus on our trials and the obstacles we would face trying to overcome them with our natural strength.

I want you to take a step of faith today. Sit down right now and vow to God a sacrificial gift as He has instructed you to do in His Word. With this you will be saying, ''God, I am worshipping You through my giving. I am offering up a thanksgiving gift of $15, $35, $50, $100, $500, $1000 or more to help You with Your business. I thank you in advance for helping me in my life.'' The Bible says that when you worship God with sacrificial thank offerings, this prepares the way for God to show you His salvation and deliver you from the troubles and trials you are facing (Psalm 50:23 NIV). Think about it. Giving to God paves the way for God to deliver you. When you give you are not buying God, but you are worshipping Him. Through your giving you are showing Him that He is your Source. Pray and ask God what you need to do to stretch your faith. Then do it today, by using the convenient form at the back of this book. Also, share with me your prayer needs, for I want to pray for you, standing in faith and believing with you. Or, if you prefer, you may call our 24-hour Prayer Ministry Center at (214) 620-6200.

You can follow the example set by the great men and women of God in history. They were great for God because they were great in faith. They were never afraid of reaching out beyond their means, vowing to God all they had. They knew the result would be a stronger, deeper faith in Him Who is the Source of our life and everything we have.

I challenge you to stretch your faith today. Look beyond your circumstances, beyond the trials you may be facing, beyond what you are and have, beyond the obstacles. Look to God, seek Him first, and trust Him with all you have. Make a vow of faith to God and fulfill it—you'll see your faith reaching heights you never dreamed of!

Remember, He gives seed to sow and bread to eat. Multiply your seed (sown). A harvest cannot come up until seed is sown. The little widow with Elijah received her abundant supply for three years because she put God's Word to work first and brought God's will as it is in Heaven into her life.

My dear friend, before you lay this book aside, make sure you put God first so you too may have the desires of your heart.

First, ask Jesus to cleanse you of your sins. You don't have to clean up your life first—God will do it for you. He will also give you a new heart, new desires, and the Spirit of truth.

If you follow these new desires—which are based on God's Word—you will have a beautiful new life on Earth, and eternal life.

Pray this prayer out loud and believe:

"Father in Heaven, I've heard Your Word, and I want to be born again. Jesus, cleanse me of my sins. I want to be a child of God. I want to give my life to You. Make me a new person. Be my Lord and Savior.

"I believe I'm now born again, because the Word of God says I am! Jesus is my Lord. Thank You, Jesus, for a new life. Amen."

Now, don't go by what you think or feel. Go by what God's Word says. You are saved—you are born again. Believe it!

If you prayed this prayer sincerely, then call us at our 24-hour prayer line—(214) 620-6200—and a prayer-minister will help you. Or, write for more information (with no obligation):

"Salvation Information"
Robert Tilton Ministries • P. O. Box 819000 • Dallas, Texas 75381
In Canada: P.O. Box 4900 • Vancouver, BC V6B 4A6

ROBERT TILTON MINISTRIES
Miracle Prayer Requests

☐ Please pray and agree with me about the pressing needs in my life.

☐ I have given unto the work of God. I believe He will open the windows of Heaven unto me, and rebuke the devourer from my life, according to Malachi 3:10-11.

☐ My specific needs are:

_____

_____

_____

_____

_____

_____

_____

RETURN THIS FOR PRAYER

Name _____

Address _____

City _____ State _____

Zip _____ Phone (_____) _____

Robert Tilton Ministries • P.O. Box 819000 • Dallas, TX 75381
In Canada: P.O. Box 4900 • Vancouver, BC V6B 4A6

If you have a testimony of how our monthly books and tapes have changed your life, please write and tell me about it. Send a snapshot of yourself, too.

_____

_____

_____

_____

_____

_____

_____

_____

_____

_____

_____

_____

_____

_____

Name _____

Address _____

City _____ State _____ Zip _____

Phone _____

Your faith makes the unseen a reality

There's nothing that Satan attacks more than our walk of faith because he knows that if he can make us doubt he can defeat us. In these exciting, in-depth lessons, Robert Tilton guides you to a greater, stronger faith by learning and using God's laws of faith.

God's Laws of Faith Course
12 audio cassettes • Study Guide

■T149 . . . . $100.00

Use order form on page 122.

Dream your impossible dream with God

Realize your vision and God's purpose in your life!

Just as a rudder gives direction to a boat, God's Word gives direction to our lives. Learn how to follow and act upon the dreams God has placed in your heart. Be and have all God created you for.

Charting Your Course by God's Dream in Your Heart

- ■T206 - 4 Audio cassettes $20.00
- ■V715 - 4 60-minute VHS videos . . $79.95

Use order form on page 122.

SUNDAY MORNING
Live

"For many years, I have been called to feed the Bread of Life to the hurting multitudes...to minister to them in the desolate spots of their lives. And now YOU can be a part of the fulfillment of that vision. Tune in every Sunday morning."

When in Dallas, visit Word of Faith Family Church located on I-35E (Valley View exit) just north of 635 (LBJ Freeway). Sunday 10 a.m. and 6 p.m.

10 AM - 12 Noon CST
Adjust your
satellite dish to
Westar 4, 10X

The Miracle Prayer Center is standing by for your call to minister to you 24 hours a day.

Call...(214) 620-6200

or, write:

Robert Tilton Ministries • P.O. Box 819000 • Dallas, TX 75381

ORDER FORM

QTY

☐ Causes and Cures of
Sin and Sickness
$30 (6 audio cassettes)

$ _____
T102

☐ God's Laws of
Faith Course
$100 (12 audio cassettes • Study Guide)

$ _____
T149

☐ Charting Your Course by
God's Dream in Your Heart
$20 (4 Audio cassettes)

$ _____
T206

$79.95 (4 60-minute VHS videos)

$ _____
V715

☐ Taking Dominion and
Exercising Authority
$19.95 (1 60-minute VHS video)

$ _____
V740

TOTAL

$ _____

Canadian Partners—Please add 20%   FOT

RETURN THIS WITH YOUR FULL PAYMENT

To make your vow call [214] 620-6200 or write:
Robert Tilton Ministries • P.O. Box 819000 • Dallas, TX 75381
In Canada: P.O. Box 4900 • Vancouver, BC V6B 4A6

Name _____

Address _____

City _____ State _____

Zip _____ Phone (_____) _____

All funds are used for designated projects and for the worldwide ministry in
accordance with Ezra 7:17-18.

ROBERT TILTON MINISTRIES
Miracle Pledge/Vow Covenant

...Pay thy vows unto the most high and call upon me in the day of trouble; I will deliver thee... **Psalms 50:14**

☐ I'm acting on this anointed word. Here's my "Prove-God Offering."

$ _____

TF-4125-500

☐ Enclosed is my offering toward my previous pledge/vow to help you in God's work.

$ _____

TF-4125-500

☐ I'm making a New "Seed of Faith Vow" of $_____. OSNL

Enclosed is my offering of:

$ _____

TF-4125-500

☐ Enclosed are my tithes to the work of God. I believe God will rebuke the devourer and open the windows of Heaven into my life.

$ _____

AA-4125-500

Upon the first day of the week let every one of you lay by him in store, as God has prospered him (I Cor. 16:2).

TOTAL

$ _____

RETURN THIS WITH YOUR VOW   FOT

To make your vow call [214] 620-6200 or write:
Robert Tilton Ministries • P.O. Box 819000 • Dallas, TX 75381
In Canada: P.O. Box 4900 • Vancouver, BC V6B 4A6

Name _____

Address _____

City _____ State _____

Zip _____ Phone (____) _____

All funds are used for designated projects and for the worldwide ministry in accordance with Ezra 7:17-18.